MIKE N

WHEN

HOW TO SEE

LIFE

THROUGH SUFFERING

HURTS

WITH BONUS BIBLE STUDY BY DR. BRUCE BECKER

Published by Straight Talk Books
P.O. Box 301, Milwaukee, WI 53201
800.661.3311 · timeofgrace.org

Printed in the United States of America
ISBN: 978-1-949488-66-1

CONTENTS

Introduction
5

Chapter 1:
Why Does God Let Me Suffer?
10

Chapter 2:
Will I Praise God Even Though I Am Hurting?
30

Chapter 3:
God, Not Again!
53

Chapter 4:
How Am I Supposed to Comfort Others?
78

Chapter 5:
God Won't Tell Me Why There's Pain?
100

Chapter 6:
God's Nonanswer Is the Answer?
123

INTRODUCTION

If you questioned my Christian faith, that wouldn't be crazy. I'm not saying that because I'm hiding some dark, sinful secret or leading some double life. I pray in church, and I pray when I'm at home. I listen to worship music and praise God in church; I do the same at home. I love opening the Bible and reading the Word of God at church; I love doing the same thing at home. But if you questioned that and asked, "Pastor Mike, but why?"— that would not be crazy.

For the past 40 years, my dad has said this to me about a thousand times: "Son, you don't know how good you've got it." That's a total dad thing to say to a kid, isn't it? "In my day, we had to . . ." "You kids these days, you don't know how good you've got it." And as much as I want to say, "Oh, okay, Dad," I stopped the other day to think about the 40 years of my life. It kind of dawned on me that he's right. I've had ups and downs; I've been through hard things and easy things. But compared to other people on this planet, I've had it pretty good. I can't relate to 71 percent of the songs on the radio because I've never had a broken heart. I met my wife, Kim, when I was in college, my first-ever girlfriend. I've never been broken up with. I've never been dumped. I've never been sepa-rated. I've never been divorced. I've had it pretty good. Besides collapsing a lung in college, I've been incredibly healthy, both physically and mentally. I've never had to battle anxiety or depression; I've never had autoimmune issues. I've had it pretty good.

I grew up in a very safe environment. I never experienced personally the wounds of trauma—not from war, not from child abuse. I've had it pretty good. Do you know what I did yesterday? I woke up at 6:00 A.M. and ran six miles with my wife while we talked about our love, our family, our blessings. I went to see one of my daughters in a volleyball tournament. She played, and the team didn't lose a single game. We hoisted the first-place trophy, picked up some pizza from Aldi on the way home, feasted as a family, read our Bible, and then together the four of us snuggled up under a fuzzy blanket to watch a documentary about Justin Bieber. So I've got it pretty good. It might not be your definition of good, but that is my definition of a great day.

WHY DO YOU BELIEVE THE THINGS YOU BELIEVE?

So if you would look at me praising God, praying to God, and grabbing my Bible, it would not be crazy of you to ask the question: "But why do you do that? Is God your heavenly vending machine—you stick in the quarters of prayer and praise because he spits out this relatively good life? Why do you believe the things you believe?"

If you're a Christian, Bible-reading person, do you ever ask yourself why? Maybe you've been through ups and downs, or maybe you are a lot like me. But it is a legit question for churchgoing people to ask. The reason I say that, and I think you'll agree with this, is because in life we realize that a person's motives matter. For example, a person can do the right thing or say the right thing outwardly, but if his heart isn't doing it for the right reason, that's not good. Right, ladies? If you're out at a bar or restaurant with your friends and a guy walks up and buys you a drink and tells you you're the prettiest girl in the place, is he a good guy? Well, you don't know yet. He's doing something outwardly nice, but what's his motive? Does he mean it? Is it for you, or is it for him? Motives matter.

Or imagine you're walking through the mall and you're having a rough day. You walk past one of those kiosks right in the middle of the aisle and the person is the nicest person you've met all week. He wants you to stop and talk. He wants to listen to you and know your name and your story. So is he the nicest person in the mall? *Hmm.* Well, you don't know yet, right? Does he just want your money? your sale? your business? your commission?

We tell our kids sometimes when they're really little, "Don't accept candy from every person who gives it to you." Grandma? Sure. Grandpa? Fine. Stranger? No. And the reason why we say that to our children is because a person's motives matter.

The exact same thing is true with God. The Bible says that God is love, and he loves us intensely. The most important commandment for people like us is to love God back with all our hearts, all our souls, all our minds, and all our strength. And because that's the case with God, our motives matter. Jesus talked about this all the time. There were people who went to church and read their Bibles and prayed and gave to the poor, but Jesus would ask questions that would get to their hearts: "Why are you doing that? Is it out of a humble, grateful, sincere love for God or not?"

This question is one of about 15 reasons why I can't wait to study the book of Job with you in this book. I'm not sure if you've read Job before, but it is a mysterious, odd, interesting, captivating, long, long, and also long book that's tucked in the Bible's Old Testament. It's about a lot of things that we talk about today. It's about why bad things happen to good people. It's about why sometimes we don't do anything wrong and everything goes wrong. It's about how we live in community in the midst of tragedy, what we say and what we shouldn't. It's about God's reasons for letting things happen to us that we don't understand completely. And it's a book that we need to study.

Before we jump into Job, however, I want to tell you what I think the book of Job is about. At its very essence, the book of Job is about the love of God. Does God really love us? If he lets certain things happen, if he knows about everything, if he has the power to control, if it would be easy for God to end all our pain and provide answers for everything we've been through, is God actually love? And at the same time, there are those questions I mentioned earlier: Why do people love God? Why would you love God? When you're on the mountaintop or you're in the darkest valley of the shadow of death, will you love God and why will you love God? We're going to explore those questions in the book of Job because the book of Job is about the love of God.

- CHAPTER 1 -
WHY DOES GOD LET ME SUFFER?

Let's start by diving right into Job chapter 1: **"In the land of Uz there lived a man whose name was Job. This man was blameless and upright; he feared God and shunned evil"** (verse 1). Bible scholars aren't exactly sure where Uz was, and they're not positive when Job lived; most people think around 2,000 B.C. But we do know this: Job was a good guy. The very first thing we read, after finding the location on the planet, is that this man was blameless and upright, he feared God, and he shunned evil—four amazing things about this one man.

This is the Bible's way of saying that Job was legit. He wasn't just a guy who put on a show at church. If you could see him behind the curtain, he was blameless and upright, no duplicity. His heart was filled with integrity. It says he feared God, which is a way of saying he was in awe of God. When he wrote the name God, he probably capitalized it. GOD was the one he believed in. And he shunned evil. When temptation knocked on his door, Job blocked it. It wasn't that Job was sinless, but it was true that Job sinned less. He was a good guy. And as we're about to find out, he had a really good life.

Check out verses 2 and 3: **"[Job] had seven sons and three daughters, and he owned seven thousand sheep, three thousand camels, five hundred yoke of oxen and five hundred donkeys, and had a large number of servants. He was the greatest man among all the people of the East."**

Job was the GOAT, right? The Greatest of Ancient Times. That's a lot of camels by the way—3,000! He had a megachurch full of just camels. If a yoke of oxen is 2 oxen, he had 11,500 animals and a large number of employees and servants. People thought of Job and said, "That's the guy." And he had 10 kids. He was an amazingly blessed man—relationally, financially, socially, culturally. The Bible says he was "the greatest man among all the peoples of the East."

And just in case you're thinking, "Wait, I know people like that—super-successful CEOs, businessowners. They are never home. Their home lives are a wreck. Their marriages are falling apart. Their kids hate them." Not Job. Look at verses 4 and 5: **"[Job's] sons used to hold feasts in their homes on their birthdays, and they would invite their three sisters to eat and drink with them. When a period of feasting had run its course, Job would make arrangements for them to be purified. Early in the morning, he would sacrifice a burnt offering for each of them, thinking, 'Perhaps my children have** sinned and cursed God in their hearts.' This was Job's regular custom."

Wow. It's a functional family. The Bible doesn't have many of those. But did you catch this? His sons held feasts in their homes on their birthdays. They had this round-robin dinner thing going. All ten of the siblings got together; they loved each other. Job was such a good father; did you notice what he did? Job didn't see his kids sinning—"Oh, my kids get wasted every time they have a birthday party." He didn't hear them sinning—"Oh, they gossiped when they all got together." No, Job said, "Perhaps my children have sinned and cursed God in their hearts." He was concerned about their relationship with God.

The details are fascinating. It says Job made arrangements; he planned on this. The first thing on his list when he got up in the morning was to sacrifice a burnt offering. In the Bible, a burnt offering was the whole animal; you just gave it to God. It was the most expensive offering. Job did this for each of his children—not just one animal for all the kids—but ten animals for all ten kids. And it says at the end of verse 5 that this was Job's "regular custom." He was a modern dad who loved his kids so much that he didn't just kiss them on the foreheads before bed; he knelt down next to their beds and prayed that they would love God with all their hearts, all their souls, all their minds, and all their strength. What did you learn in the first five verses of the book of Job?

Job is a very good guy who has a very good life.

But then the plot takes a twist. In perhaps the oddest scene in the Bible, we read this: **"One day the angels came to present themselves before the Lord, and Satan also came with them. The Lord said to Satan, 'Where have you come from?' Satan answered the Lord, 'From roaming throughout the earth, going back and forth on it.' Then the Lord said to Satan, 'Have you considered my servant Job? There's no one on earth like him; he is blameless and upright, a man who fears God and shuns evil'"** (verses 6–8).

And half the Christians say, "What?! Wait, no. God's in heaven, right? And all the angels are around him praising and worshiping. That makes sense to me. And Satan came with them? What? Isn't Satan down in hell, really distant from God's presence in heaven?" Those are good questions. This is a really deep, really interesting rabbit hole, and here's the gist of it: It turns out in the Bible that God is so powerful that he occasionally holds staff meetings with all the good, holy angels and all the fallen ones. The good ones love God and trust God; the fallen ones don't. But God, in his power and in his plans, uses all of them to bless people like you.

The good ones are sent out as servants; the evil ones, in their deceptions and lies, think they're going to trip up God's people, but he has a bigger plan. It happens in the book of Job, and it actually happened with Jesus himself. Do you remember who filled Judas' heart to betray Jesus?

Satan did. And after the betrayal, what happened? God crushed Satan's head and forgave your sins and rescued you so you could be with God in paradise forever. God is controlling everything. It's not a yin-yang thing, good vs. evil; it's God here, and everything else there.

But what I want to get into is how incredibly proud God was of his servant Job. Did you catch that? God was the one who brought Job into the conversation. "Satan, where have you been? Roaming around in the earth? Huh. Did you see Job? My servant Job is blameless and upright, he fears me, and he shuns evil." That's amazing to think about. God was in heaven, surrounded by angels, and he was boasting about his beloved child Job. Right now God's not just running the universe and keeping stars from crashing into each other; he's actually talking with angelic beings about his servants on earth. And here he said, "Satan, you see this guy? He loves me. And I love him." The book of Job is about the love of God, and Job does love God because God loved him first.

GOD IS CONTROLLING EVERYTHING.

In Hebrew, Satan is literally "the satan," and *Satan* in Hebrew means "enemy" or "adversary." Satan wasn't going to say amen to this gushfest between God and his dear servant Job. He was going to sow seeds of doubt, and that's what he did next: **"'Does Job fear God for nothing?' Satan replied. 'Have you not put a hedge around him and his household and everything he has? You have** blessed the work of his hands, so that his flocks and herds are spread throughout the land. But now stretch out your hand and strike everything he has, and he will surely curse you to your face'" (verses 9-11).

Essentially, Satan asked, "But why? Oh, I see your servant, God. Yep, he serves you. He offers sacrifices, one for each kid, but why does he do it, God? It's not because he loves you; it's because he's using you. You've set up this hedge, this tall fence around Job's life, and everything is good inside and everything is bad outside. Why wouldn't he praise you?"

One Bible paraphrase says that Satan said to God, "God, you pamper him like your pet. So he sits and he stays because he knows he's about to get a treat, right? You put up the hedge. There's poverty out there, but rich Job in here. There are dysfunctional families out there, but not Job's in here. Of course he praises you; who wouldn't praise you if they get that much back? But I'll tell you what, God. Let's make a deal, God. Strike him, and we'll see what's in his heart. Decrease his blessings, and he will increase his cursing. And he will not perhaps say it in his heart; he will say it, God, right to your face. Increase his pain, and Job will decrease his praise."

And God, shockingly, said, "Deal." Verse 12: "The Lord said to Satan, 'Very well, then, everything Job has is in your power, but on the man himself do not lay a finger.' Then Satan went out from the presence of the Lord." And in this chapter, we're going to see exactly what Satan did to Job. We're going to see exactly how Job reacts to God, hashtag #you'vegottocomeback.

For now, though, I want you to highlight this big idea. It's the idea that God and Satan both agree upon: *Pain proves it.* If you're in my boat, you can pray and you can praise; you can give, you can gather, and you can put down Jesus roots. That's all good, but it's not proven. It's only when God allows pain and someone reacts with praise that faith is proven.

The New Testament book of 1 Peter, written by Jesus' close friend Peter, actually talks a lot about this. It's about suffering sometimes when it's not your fault. And in 1 Peter 1:7, Peter says when you go through the fire and the trials and the grief and you still hold on to Jesus, it proves the genuineness of your faith. You've got to know that you're not using God when God takes and you still praise.

That's why in this chapter I want to write directly to those who are not in my boat. It's for those who can't say it was a great day yesterday. For those who know the sting and the sorrow and the grief and who fight back the tears most days of the week.

One of the bittersweet things about being a pastor is I hear about so much of the pain. I think about the couples who have miscarried recently. They had big dreams and hopes to start a family, and then God said, "No." I think about the people, the massive numbers of people at my church, who have endured trauma. They went to serve our country and came home with nightmares and flashbacks they can't control and find themselves reaching for a bottle of pills. They prayed, and God hasn't fixed it. I think of all the people who know what it's like to say, "I'll love you no matter what," and then it doesn't work out. There's the pain of divorce and the bitterness of separation and the heartbreak of being stuck in the messy middle of a marriage that isn't what they thought it would be. I think of those who have been abused in their lives, verbally or emotionally or sexually. I think about how that affects people.

I think about the young couple from our church who for almost their entire marriage has been dealing with cancer. They've been dealing with chemo and with sickness and with surgery. I think of those who have depression that hangs over their heads like a cloud all the time. And while I lament that and pray about it and love it when they reach out for help, there's something I will say about the pain. It proves it. If they are still worshiping in church, if they are lifting up the name of Jesus and saying, "Christ be magnified," they proved it.

I'll put it this way: Imagine a bandaged hand represents the brokenness of your life. Imagine the bandage is the pain, the sorrow, the addiction, and the heartache. If you fold that bandaged hand with your other hand to pray, you prove it. If you raise your bandaged hand as you sing praise to God, you prove it. If you go to church, shake hands with others, gather in Jesus' name even though life has been hard, you prove it. If you give an offering to God even though you don't have much, you prove it.

If you've been through brokenness, limped your way into church, and yet you still love God, you proved it. Satan would love to slander God all day long; he would love to say that you're using God for something good. He'd love to say that your faith is fake and that God isn't worthy of praise. But every time you open the Bible in the midst of your pain, you prove it. When you walk into church, you shut the devil's mouth. When you limp into church, you prove that God is worthy of your love. When you sing at the end of your hardest days, you prove that God is worthy. You are proving that Satan is the father of lies and God is a Father who's worthy of all praise.

GOD IS A FATHER WHO'S WORTHY OF ALL PRAISE.

I hate your pain. And I love it, because the one thing you and I want more than anything is to say, "God, you are worthy of everything."

A while ago, a five-year-old boy from my church was raking leaves with his grandma in the middle of a beautiful, sunny day. He tripped and fell right into the fire. Grandma picked him up, but he was burned. It was bad. He was rushed to the hospital, and the doctors stuck this little boy in an ambulance to try to ease his pain and get him to the burn unit in Madison. When he got there—this little kid, in pain, having fallen into the fire—do you know what he said? "Jesus will heal me." Five years old.

Maybe you've never felt the fire of pain and suffering. But maybe you have been in the fire. Maybe you have the scars from that suffering. You can say, like this little brother in Christ, "Jesus will heal me. He's enough. He is here right now. I'm not going to turn on God. I'm not going to accuse him. No, I know he is with me. He can allow this pain. He can permit it. He can ruin me. He can slay me, but I will praise him today." I hope you do too. Even though the divorce happened. Even though the cancer might kill you. Even though you miss her so much. Even though you wish you could go back and undo what happened to you. Even though . . . I will, you will . . . because God is all that we need.

How do you do that—keep trusting God, keep praising him—despite struggle? I don't know when it's coming for me, but it's coming. There's going to be a day—it might be tomorrow or 30 years from now—a time when I don't have it so good. How do you and I prepare for that next moment of pain?

I want to end this chapter with a quick clue. Read over Job 1:1-12 again. These incredible verses from the Bible contain something powerful. Let me show you: God, God, Lord, Lord, Lord, Lord, God, God, Lord, Lord. Did you catch that before? Highlight the words so you see them even better: *God, God, Lord, Lord, Lord, Lord, God, God, Lord, Lord.* Ten times in this half chapter of the Bible we hear about God. And if you knew Hebrew, you would say, "Whoa!" The Hebrew name for *God, Elohim,* implies power, might, strength. The Hebrew word for *Lord,* some Bibles put it in all capital letters, is *Yahweh, Jehovah.* It means "I Am." It means the God of love, the God who keeps his promises, the God who is always there for us. At the very start of the most painful book of the Bible, we see Elohim, the God of power, and Yahweh, the God of love. Put those two together and find a God who is worthy of praise.

Satan would love to tell you the next time that pain happens, "God's so powerful, right? He's running the show, but does he love you? He's God; he could stop it. He could cure cancer like that or fix sick kids or fix everything. He's so powerful, so why doesn't he do it for you? He doesn't love you; you shouldn't love him back." And when that comes, do you know what you're going to say to Satan? "Pain proves it. My God is not just the God of almighty power who sits enthroned in heaven. My God is the God of the cross, and he proved it. Two thousand years ago, Jesus came to this world and didn't stay in a supernatural force field that kept brokenness outside and blessing inside. Instead, he went through pain for me. The nails proved it. The crown proved it. The cross proved it."

Every time you and I wonder in the midst of our suffering and pain, "Does God love me?" we fix our eyes on Jesus and say, "He must because pain proves it. He can't be using me for my money, my time, my prayers, my praise. Who would go through something like that unless it was love?"

Because of that love, as one of my friends recently wrote, "There is a conversation going on in heaven right now about you, and it is incredibly kind." I don't know if Satan showed up for an all-angel staff meeting today, but I wonder

HE LOVED US FIRST.

if God said, "Have you seen my servant? She has cancer, and she came to church. He went through a divorce, and he prayed to me today. She's a victim of abuse, but she still believes that I am good. He fell into the fire. She has battled addiction. They know what it's like to suffer, and look where they are. Have you seen my servants? They love me. And I gave them a good reason to."

Pain proves it. Our pain proves we love God. God's pain proves that he loved us first.

PRAYER

Dear Lord, you are worthy of all glory and honor and praise. I am here today, maybe at the highest high or maybe at the lowest low, but I am saying you are worthy of glory and honor and praise. God, I don't always get you. I feel like if I had control of all the buttons and levers, I would do things so much differently than you do, but I'm not you. I know nothing, and you know everything. So in humility I take a knee before the cross and say, "Your will be done." And I will lift up your name because I believe you're worthy of it. You are the God who has all the power in the world, yet you subdued that power when your Son died on a cross.

Jesus, you are the one who walked on the waves. You raised people from the dead. But on the cross, Jesus, you did nothing to lessen your pain and suffering; you did not intervene on your own behalf. You did it to prove your love for me. Thank you, God, for your forgiveness and grace for my sins. Thank you that the blood of Jesus covers up all my doubts and questions and the moments when I turned on you. Thank you that if I call upon the glorious name of Jesus today, I can be sure that I will end up in a place where there is no brokenness, no pain, no tears, and no illness. Thank you for the hope of heaven, and thank you for being with me while I am here on earth. As I study this book of Job, God, keep your love ever before me. I pray all these things in your powerful name. Amen.

FOR FURTHER STUDY: WHY DOES GOD LET ME SUFFER?

DR. BRUCE BECKER

According to Pastor Mike, what is the book of Job about?

In chapter 1, Pastor Mike addressed God's purpose in allowing pain in our lives. But before we dig deeper into the teaching, let's consider some of the background to the book of Job that Pastor Mike referenced.

In Job chapter 1, we learn about a man named Job who lives in Uz: **"In the land of Uz there lived a man whose name was Job"** (verse 1).

Have you ever wondered if Job was a real-life human being or just a character in a made-up story? Is the book of Job a historical account or just a super-long work of fiction designed to teach a spiritual lesson on pain, patience, and perseverance? These are questions that people have asked throughout the ages.

We get some help answering these questions from three other places in the Bible (outside the book of Job) that mention Job by name. Two are in the book of Ezekiel, and the third one is in the book of James.

> The word of the LORD came to me: "Son of man, if a country sins against me by being unfaithful and I stretch out my hand against it to cut off its food supply and send famine upon it and kill its people and their animals, even if these three men—Noah, Daniel and Job—were in it, they could save only themselves by their righteousness, declares the Sovereign LORD. (Ezekiel 14:12-14)

> Or if I send a plague into that land and pour out my wrath on it through bloodshed, killing its people and their animals, as surely as I live, declares the Sovereign LORD, even if Noah, Daniel and Job were in it, they could save neither son nor daughter. They would save only themselves by their righteousness. (Ezekiel 14:19,20)

> Brothers and sisters, as an example of patience in the face of suffering, take the prophets who spoke in the name of the Lord. As you know, we count as blessed those who have persevered. You have heard of Job's perseverance and have seen what the Lord finally brought about. The Lord is full of compassion and mercy. (James 5:10,11)

Based on these three sections of Scripture, how would

you answer the question of whether Job was a fictional character or a historical person?

―――――

"In the land of Uz" sounds eerily similar to "the land of Oz" from the classic movie the *Wizard of Oz*. In the movie, Oz is a fantasyland filled with munchkins, flying monkeys, witches, and three unique companions who accompanied Dorothy to find the wizard.

So what about the land of Uz? Was it a make-believe place or an actual geographical location? We get some help answering these questions from two other places in the Bible. One is in the book of Jeremiah. The other is in the book of Lamentations.

In Jeremiah 25:15-26, there is a list of places and people upon whom the Lord would bring judgment. Jeremiah was to give each of them a "cup of wrath" from the hand of the Lord. The list includes Jerusalem, Judah, Pharaoh king of Egypt and all the Egyptian people, the kings of Uz, all the kings of the Philistines, Edom, Moab, and many others.

In Lamentations 4:21, Jeremiah delivers a similar message of judgment on the people of Edom because of their failure to worship and serve the Lord: **"Rejoice and be glad, Daughter Edom, you who live in the land of Uz. But to you also the cup will be passed."**

Based on these two sections of Scripture, how would you answer the question of whether Uz was a make-believe place or an actual geographical location?

―――――

Pastor Mike described Job as the GOAT—The Greatest of Ancient Times. Can you identify four or five characteristics/realities in Job's life that made him the greatest man in ancient times?

1.

2.

3.

4.

5.

―――――

Pastor Mike indicated that he didn't have time to address the question of why or how Satan showed up one day with the Lord's angels. Let's explore the question here: **"One day the angels came to present themselves before the Lord, and Satan also came with them. The Lord said to Satan, 'Where have you come from?' Satan answered the Lord, 'From roaming throughout the earth, going back and forth on it'"** (Job 1:6,7).

Based on these two verses, what are the two places where Satan has the ability to travel?

This leads us to two related questions: What does Satan do when he travels around the earth? and What does Satan do when he shows up before the Lord in heaven? Pastor Mike explained that Satan is our enemy, or adversary. He has no interest in our well-being, so he's definitely not traveling the earth to determine how he can help us. So what's he doing?

There is another term that the Bible uses to describe Satan and his enemy activities. The word is *accuser*. Read Revelation 12:10: **"Now have come the salvation and the power and the kingdom of our God, and the authority of his Messiah. For the accuser of our brothers and sisters, who accuses them before our God day and night, has been hurled down."**

How often does Satan engage in the activity of making accusations?

When Satan roams the earth, what is he looking for from among the "brothers and sisters" (believers in Jesus) that he can bring before God?

In Job 1:8, the Lord has a suggestion for Satan as he's roaming the earth: **"Have you considered my servant Job? There is no one on earth like him; he is blameless**

and upright, a man who fears God and shuns evil."

In your own words, what was the Lord saying about Job?

———

Satan had already considered the Lord's servant Job in his worldwide travels because he made an accusation about Job.

What was Satan's accusation about Job? (Job 1:9,10)

———

What was Satan's suggestion to the Lord? What was Satan's expectation if the Lord did as Satan suggested? (Job 1:11)

———

How did the Lord respond to Satan's suggestion? (Job 1:12)

———

Put yourself in Job's sandals. What if this wasn't the book of Job we're reading but the book of _____ (insert your first name)? How would you answer the following questions?

> When Satan roams the earth and comes across you living out your life, what accusations might he take back to the Lord about you?

When the Lord hears the accusations of Satan about you, how do you think that conversation would go? How do you think the Lord would respond? Before you answer these questions, read Zechariah 3:1-10 and first consider the following questions for yourself or discuss them with others in your group:

Whom was Satan accusing on this occasion?

What did Joshua's filthy clothes represent?

Who is the "Branch" who was referred to in verse 8? (For a giveaway hint, read Jeremiah 23:5,6.)

What is the connection between the Branch and Joshua getting clean clothes to wear?

With Job and Joshua in mind, you can now answer the question: How do you think the Lord would respond to Satan's accusations about you?

What is the most significant takeaway from chapter 1 for you?

– CHAPTER 2 –

WILL I PRAISE GOD EVEN THOUGH I AM HURTING?

If you were the devil, how would you do it?

I know that's a serious question to start a chapter with. But if you were the devil, how would you do it? We sometimes think of the devil and demons as being these dark forces that try to freak us out horror-movie style, keep us up at night, and bump in the darkness, but that's not at all biblical. Read the Bible, and you'll find out that Satan's greatest goal, the thing that he stays up at night plotting and planning, is simply this: to separate you and God from a relationship that is defined by love. This idea that God is love; that God loves the world; that God gave his Son; that our sins are forgiven and it means so much to us that we want to love God back with our whole hearts, souls, minds, and strength . . . that's the thing Satan wants to get into the middle of.

He doesn't really care how he does it. He can make you super bitter at church and religion and God. Or he can just make you super busy with really good things that get in the way of the best thing. But he does care intensely that he does it. He cares that people just like you don't go to bed tonight thinking, "God is so loving, and I love God so much." There's a dozen different forms and tactics that Satan might use, but I think if you look at history, you'd have to say that one of his most effective strategies ever has been pain.

Sometimes pain drives people to the Bible and to prayer, but what often happens—and I bet it's happened to you—is that pain becomes a question mark on the love of God, right? It's actually very logical; I understand why the tactic works. If someone has all the resources and power to fix your problem and they just sit back and don't help, you've got to start asking yourself the question, "Well, do they really love me?" And so this biblical idea that God loves us and is also almighty and all-powerful doesn't always make sense when we're in pain. "If God is so powerful and so loving, why would I go through something this difficult?"

I thought of that struggle when I read the things many people in my congregation sent to me. A while back, a survey was sent to the members of my church family, and the survey had two questions on it. Question one: What's the hardest thing you've ever been through in life? Question two: What happened to your view of God when that thing happened? Seventy-seven members of the church family replied, and I read story after story after story after story after story after story.

Do you know what the hardest stories were to read?

The ones about relationships. Reflecting back on life, some people said the hardest things were when business didn't work out, when they couldn't pay their bills. That came up once, twice, maybe three times. And lots of people talked about physical stuff: the cancer came back, the struggles with their bodies and the pain, the hospitalization; that was very real. But the thing that was most heartbreaking was to read the times when God didn't fix the relationships that mattered most. You know, when you want to find love and can't. Or you think you found love, and then it doesn't work out. When you want to start a family, but you're infertile. Or God gives you a family, and then you miscarry.

I think a lot of us, deep down, just want great friendships, great relationships. We want to be close with our parents, we want to find love, and maybe lots of us want to have children. When that doesn't happen and when you ask God not once or twice but you beg him for years and he doesn't fix it, then you ask the question, "Seriously? You're the God who can part the seas. You can turn water into wine. You can speak and people exist, but you can't just push a button and bless me?" It's a huge struggle in a world like this with lives like ours to believe from your first day until your last one the most basic sentence of the Bible: God is love. Period.

So either you've been through something really painful, or you're right in the midst of it now and don't have to think hard to apply this to your life. Or maybe it's going to happen before this year is over. When life is hard for you, what will you do? What will you say to yourself to push back and resist one of the devil's greatest goals?

I really want to prepare you because this is the question that sends some people closer to God, and it pushes many people further and further away from God. There are some people who, because of the pain of life, have ended up not just disillusioned with God but complete atheists who deny his existence. I realize what's at stake, and I want to save you from that temptation. To do so, I want to turn to the words of a man who suffered probably more than you and me combined: an Old Testament guy named Job.

WHEN LIFE IS HARD FOR YOU, WHAT WILL YOU DO?

In the last chapter, I covered what the book of Job is all about. Do you remember? The book of Job is about the love of God. It's about what happens when life is really, really hard. "Will I still love God, or am I just doing all this church stuff because he's made life easy? Will I love God in the ups and the downs? Does God love me? If he's allowing this, permitting this, sending this, is he really the God of love whom he claims to be?" The book of Job is about those two related things. It's about the love of God, and that's why I want to dive back into it with you.

A quick review: Job lived sometime around the time of Abraham, 2,000 B.C. He had one wife, three daughters, seven sons, and thousands of animals. He was a good man with great faith. Satan showed up and said to God, "But does he seriously love you? I mean, you pamper Job like your pet, right? Sure he sits, he stays, and he obeys. You've given him the greatest life of anyone whom I know. But, God, I bet if you take the good life away, he will curse you to your face." And God, bafflingly, says, "Deal." And that's where we pick things up.

"One day when Job's sons and daughters were feasting and drinking wine at the oldest brother's house, a messenger came to Job and said, 'The oxen were plowing and the donkeys were grazing nearby, and the Sabeans attacked and made off with them. They put the servants to the sword, and I am the only one who has escaped to tell you!'" (Job 1:13-15).

The Sabeans were ancient desert nomads; they lived in modern-day Yemen or Saudi Arabia. They swept up probably on their camels, and they took away 1,500 of Job's animals; over 10 percent of his net worth was gone in an instant. And even worse, all the servants except one—employees whom godly Job loved, blessed, and prayed for—were all dead. And one guy—sweaty, broken, confused—ran to Job with the news.

"While he was still speaking, another messenger came and said, 'The fire of God fell from the heavens and burned up the sheep and the servants, and I am the only one who has escaped to tell you!'" (verse 16). Fire of God? Was it a meteor? a lightning storm? a supernatural Sodom and Gomorrah kind of moment? We don't know, but we know it wasn't man-made; it came from the heavens. All seven thousand sheep were gone in an instant. Over 50 percent of Job's net worth was destroyed, and these innocent servants were scorched and killed by the fire that fell from heaven.

"While he was still speaking, another messenger came and said, 'The Chaldeans formed three raiding parties and swept down on your camels and made off with them. They put the servants to the sword, and I am the only one who has escaped to tell you!'" (verse 17).

The Sabeans lived in the south; the Chaldeans lived in the north, a kind of Babylon of the ancient world. They had a plan. They divided, they conquered, they took all three thousand camels, and they murdered every servant but a single one. Now all Job's animals, his entire business, and almost all his servants and employees were dead and gone. I wish that was the worst part. And Job did too.

"While he was still speaking, yet another messenger came and said, 'Your sons and daughters were feasting and drinking wine at the oldest brother's house, when suddenly a mighty wind swept in from the desert and struck the four corners of the house. It collapsed on them and they are dead, and I am the only one who has escaped to tell you!'" (verses 18,19).

Satan licked his lips; angels, who do not know the future, held their breath. Job was a God-fearing man, but God had given him the greatest life of anyone around. Now that that life, in an instant, was completely gone, would he fear God? Would he love him? Would he praise him? Would he shake his fist at the heavens, at the God who could have stopped it but didn't? Or would he fall on his knees and worship? All of heaven held its breath, and all of hell did too. What would Job do?

It reminds me of the story of Tia Coleman. You might remember this. In 2018 Tia Coleman, her entire immediate family, and a bunch of her extended family took a vacation. Near Branson, Missouri, they posed for a classic tourist picture in front of a green screen (you can see the picture online). They all smiled, and then they got on a boat—a boat that was able to travel on land and water—and they were enjoying it. The tour guide said, "The life jackets are down there, but you won't need them." A storm came out of nowhere, waves swelled up on the lake, they came over the front of the boat, and it sunk. And 17 people, including 9 people from Tia's family, died. Her husband died. Her nine-year-old died. Her seven-year-old died. And her one-year-old baby died. She barely survived herself, and when she came up from the water, rescue workers revived her. She wished she had died too. In a Job-like moment, her entire life had changed. Now what would she do?

Previously, Tia had been an active member of her Christian church, a church in Indianapolis. She used to show up, lift her hands in praise, fold her hands in prayer, and look to Jesus as this incredible God and Savior, but what would she do now? And what would Job do? Messenger after messenger after messenger after messenger came; how would he react to the tragic news? Answer: Incredibly. Look at verse 20: **"At this, Job got up and tore his robe and shaved his head."** He grieved.

If anyone ever tells you in the Christian church you're just supposed to clap and smile and praise God because he is good, it's not biblically true. Jesus wept, and Job lamented; he tore his robe like people in that culture did to show outwardly what he felt like in his heart, which had been torn apart. He shaved his head; he collapsed with nothing.

But he still had everything. Verse 20 continues: **"Then Job fell to the ground in worship."** The word *worship* simply means saying to God, "You're worth it." Do you go to church regularly on Sunday? You could be doing a million other things. Why do you go? Not just because of the coffee, right? You go because you believe that God is worth it. It's worth it to hear his Word. It's worth it to sing his praises. Why do you do it? Because God is worth it! He stirs your heart, and he saved you from your sins. He rose from the dead. Do you give offerings even though you don't have a ton of money in the bank? Why do you do **GOD IS WORTH IT.** that? Because he's worth it. Because you believe God is so good, so merciful, so patient, and so loving that you gather to worship. In the midst of his lament and pain, that's exactly what Job did. He said, "God, you're worth it. My heart is torn apart, but you are still worthy of my praise."

Which begs this massive question: How could he think that? I mean, you can blame human free will if the Sabeans and Chaldeans take all your animals. But who controls the fire from the sky or the wind that sweeps in from the desert? That's God. How can you say, "God, you're worth it" when he is the one directly or indirectly sovereign and in control over the pain that you've been through?

Now in the next paragraph, I'm going to show you Job's answer to that question. But I've got to tell you that what Job is about to say is not what I would say to you. If you lost a kid today, if there was a car accident and you lost loved ones today, if you were going through tragedy and you came brokenhearted into my office, I think what I would say to you are two things. I would say God is still here, and God is going to take you there. I know you're hurting. I grieve with you, but God is close to the brokenhearted (Psalm 34:18). God is here in the midst of the trouble. The world is falling apart, but God is constant. I would tell you that. I would say that as much as this hurts, it will not hurt forever. God is going to take you to a place, heaven, where there's no pain or grief or funerals or mourning or crying or tragedy or confusion. You're going to get through this because God is here. This is going to end, and eternal happiness will begin. That's what I would say to you in the midst of your suffering, but that is not what Job said. He didn't fall to the ground in worship and say, "God, thank you for still being here even though my kids aren't." He didn't say, "God, I'm worshiping you today because you promise me eternal life where I won't feel like this forever." That's not what Job said. What he said is incredible.

"[Job] fell to the ground in worship and said: 'Naked I came from my mother's womb, and naked I will depart. The Lord gave and the Lord has taken away; may the name of the Lord be praised.' In all this, Job did not sin by charging God with wrongdoing" (verses 20-22).

You catch that? Job didn't sin; he wiped the smirk off Satan's face. He didn't say, "God, you did me wrong. Seriously, why did you?" He didn't do any of that. Instead, he worshiped. He praised God's name, and here's his rationale: "Because I came in naked, and it's the same way I'm going out." In other words, Job kind of zoomed back from that little slice of pain and looked at his entire life and said, "You know what, when I was born, I came in buck naked." Job's momma didn't push him out with Job holding three thousand camels. He came in with nothing: no net worth, no massive flocks and herds. Job was not a little kid who was born with ten of his own kids. He came into the world with nothing, and to Job, logically, that meant that God had given him everything. If he had a family, it was because of God. If he had children, it was because of God. If he had sheep or camels or oxen or whatever, God had chosen to give it. The Lord gave, Job confessed, and he takes away.

At the end of our lives, we can't take anything with us. There will be no U-Haul on the back of the hearse. You and I will be stripped naked and washed clean. Someone will comb our hair, put us in our favorite outfit, and put us in a box. We can't take anything with us. Naked you come in, naked you go out, and everything in between those two naked days is up to God. He gives it, and he can take it.

This is what some Christians call the teaching of stewardship. Have you heard that word before? *Stewardship* is just a fancy way of saying that if there's anything good in your life, you don't own it; God is just letting you manage it. Do you have shoes on your feet? Do you have money in your bank account? Do you have good health and strength? Do you have a business that you own? a family that you're caring for? That's not your stuff; God gave it. You didn't come into this world with it; that means that God gave it. And if God owns it, he has every right to take it back. That is the baseline belief that will save you from bitterness and anger and questioning the love of the God who is love.

To illustrate this, think about your phone. Say you left your phone at home but you need to make a call. You ask your friend if you can use her phone, and she says, "Sure!" When you're done, you don't keep the phone, right? She asks for it back. You have no right to keep her phone.

Now what if that phone represents everything good that God gives? Naked you and I come into this world, and anything we get is us saying, "God, would you please?" In his kindness and love, he says, "Sure." And when he says, "Can I have that back?" it's illogical to say, "Who do you think you are?" He says, "It's mine, and so I can give you the gift or I can take it away." As Job so beautifully said, "The LORD gave and the LORD has taken away; may the name of the LORD be praised." And if you do this, like Job, you will not sin by charging God with wrongdoing.

GIVE GOD THE RIGHT TO GIVE OR TO TAKE AWAY.

The key that Job learned from suffering is this: *Give God the right.* Make a decision right now in your heart and mind to give God the right to give or to take away, to bless you abundantly or to do so sparingly. Give God the right, and you won't accuse God of doing you wrong.

It's actually what Tia did. Remember Tia Coleman from the tragic boating accident? Eight days after her life was barely spared, her church had a funeral service for her immediate family. Grace Apostolic Church in Indianapolis hosted a service with four white caskets in front of the church: her husband, her nine-year-old, her seven-year-old, and her baby. And Tia sat right there in the front row. Her pastor came and opened a Bible, and her extended family came. Her friends and the choir members were all there, and they sang the praises of Jesus. They read the words of Jesus. They cried out from their broken hearts to the heart of Jesus. But the truth was that those people were not Tia. They would go home to their families. They would go home to beds that were warm from the bodies of their partners. They would go home to toys strewn about and kids being crazy. Tia would not. She would go home to quiet. So what would she do?

Answer: She worshiped. During the three-hour funeral service, Tia was often seen raising her hands to worship Jesus, folding her hands to ask Jesus for help, crying out to the beautiful name of Jesus, just like Job. In the midst of her lament and praise, she said, "God can give, and God can take away. May the name of God be praised."

So here's the question: Will you give God the right? Your answer to that question and the extent to which you answer it will determine the closeness of your loving relationship with God. Today, as hard as it would be, as unthinkable as it is to think about, will you give God the right to all of it? "God, I want to have a good day today. Please. But if I don't, you have the right. God, I want this lump to be nothing. But if it isn't? I give you the right. God, I want my marriage to get through this. I'm going to do everything I can to help with that. But if it doesn't work? If I'm googling the number of the nearest lawyer, I give you the right. I want people to be nice to my kids in school but even if they're not, even if it's a hard experience, God you have the right. Give me money; then take it. Give me health; then take it. Give me love; then take it. Give me everything, or give me nothing. At the end of the day, God, you have the right."

Will you believe that? If not, I don't know what to tell you. And if you do, I'm so happy for you because you will be prepared through all the ups and downs of life to worship and praise the one constant presence in your life: God.

Now if that freaks you out—and I'm sensing it does—
let me give you just one little bit of help. Actually, Job is
going to give you a little bit of help. There's something
you might not know about the book of Job. In the book
of Job, there are two primary names used for God. In Hebrew, the word that we translate "God" is *Elohim*, and it
has the connotation of power, strength, and might. And
then there's this other name used for God, the Lord, it's
sometimes in all capitals; it's the word *Yahweh*. And it
means "I Am." God just is. He's present. He's constant.
He makes a promise and then keeps it. For almost all of
the book of Job, the name Yahweh, the Lord, is never used,
especially when Job and his friends argue for 35 straight
chapters. There it's just, "God, God, God, God, God, God,
God, power, power, power, power. Why, God, why? Why,
God, why? Why, God, why?" But in the opening of Job and
in his response, when he thinks about the God who has
taken everything, did you notice what he called him?

Let me show you. Job said, **"The Lord gave and the
Lord has taken away; may the name of the Lord be
praised."** Yahweh, Yahweh, Yahweh. I Am. I Am the
promise-keeping God, the promise-keeping God, the
promise-keeping God. It's almost as if Job is only able to
worship at the bottom because he knows there is a God
who will be there with him.

You can believe that too. And if you're struggling, if
you're in the midst of that pain, if your love and passion

for God are a flickering flame that's about to be snuffed out, I just want you to think about the connections between that Jesus and this Job.

Jesus was the greatest too. He didn't have 11,500 animals; he had 10,000 times 10,000 angels. He was the greatest in the kingdom of God, and yet he gave it all up. Two thousand years ago in the little town of Bethlehem, Jesus was born naked from his mother, Mary. And 33 years later, he would die naked on a Roman cross. His Father had given it to him, and his Father took it away. Jesus grieved. Job tore his robe. Jesus had his robe stripped from him. Job shaved his head. Jesus' head was crowned with a crown of thorns. Jesus, like Job, had questions for God: "Why, God? Why, God?" And yet, just like Job, Jesus didn't accuse his Father of doing him wrong. He didn't sin. Instead, he suffered *for you*.

The good news of the Bible is that Jesus went through that. He praised God even in the midst of the storm so that you would know this: God is not just the one who owns everything. God is the one who has done everything so that you and he would be together forever. If this week is the hardest week you've had in a long time, you can say, "But God is here, and he's coming back soon. I'm going to get through this with his help, one day at a time, and then one day will come when I will see his face and be so glad I didn't turn on him." And Satan will wail as you stand in faith and strength and believe in the depth of your soul. God is not just God. It's not the "Judge gives and the Judge takes." It's the *Lord*. My Savior. A God who must be so great.

For your sake, your soul's sake, your family's sake, give God the right. Just like my mom did. Do you know why I'm a pastor? Because when I was a teenager, I was reading my Bible at home like I did every day, and there was just something Jesus said that made me want to be a pastor. So I did. And you'd say, "Well, why were you reading your Bible at home? Most teenage boys play video games, not read their Bibles. Why were you reading yours?" And the answer would be because we had this pastor at our church who really inspired me to come to church and want to read the Bible. And you'd say, "Wow, well, how'd you end up at that church?" And the answer is, "My mom." I'm super blessed right now because my mom and my dad and my mother-in-law and my wife and my kids all go to my church. But back in those days, it was just Judy. You've heard of Judge Judy; this was Just Judy. Judy bringing me. Judy sometimes dragging me. Judy keeping me connected. If you're a Christian mom, I thank God for you.

But here's something you don't know; something my mom gave me permission to share with you. My mom had to give God the right. I was raised as the youngest kid in my family, but technically I'm not the youngest kid. I have no memory of him, but I've seen pictures of me holding him, my little brother, Jimmy. James was born really sick, and he only stayed on this earth for six weeks. My parents had wanted another kid. God had given, and then way too quickly, God took. And my mom had been raised as a Jesus-loving, churchgoing, prayer-praying woman, but now she faced the hardest thing in her entire life; she lost a child. What would she do? And the answer

HE'S THE LORD. is she praised God for me, for us; she gave God the right. She called the pastor. She ran to the church. As she would tell me in a recent text, "I had nowhere else to go but God."

In her grief, my mom worshiped Jesus. And because she did, I know Jesus. And now, through all the ups and downs I've been through in life, I know I have Jesus. I'm asking you, I'm hoping for you, I'm pleading with you to give God the right. He's not just God; he's the Lord. And you know he has to be good because of what he did for you.

PRAYER

Dear God, the father of lies does not want me to believe the truth. There's something in my life—maybe he knows already what it is—that I think I own. I think it's mine, and even you, God, don't have the right to touch it. God, as much as I don't want to think about that, help me to think about it and to confess it. You can take it, God. I'm praying today that you don't take it, but if you do, I still love you because I know how deeply you love me.

Thank you, Jesus, for everything you've given me. If it wasn't

for the cross, I would always have a good reason to question why. I'd have a reason to question your love and character, but the fact that you did that for me despite my doubts, despite my sins, despite my struggles, God, the fact that you did that for a sinful person is the best proof in human history that you must be love. And so I hold on to your heart today. I do believe in you. Now help me overcome my unbelief. It's in Jesus' name that I boldly and joyfully pray. Amen.

FOR FURTHER STUDY: WILL I PRAISE GOD EVEN THOUGH I AM HURTING?

DR. BRUCE BECKER

In preparation for this second chapter, Pastor Mike sent out a survey to the members of his local church family. The survey had just two questions. Consider these questions for yourself, or discuss them with others in your group:

1. What's the hardest thing you've ever been through in life?

2. What happened to your view of God when that thing happened?

The Lord had given Satan permission "to strike everything Job had." The fact that Satan needed the Lord's permission indicates something about the Lord and something about Satan.

What does it indicate about the Lord and who he is?

What does it indicate about Satan and his power over our lives?

What assurance does this reality about Satan give us?

———

On a single day, Job experienced four tragic losses within his family, among his workers, and with his possessions. Two were the result of what other people (creatures) did, and two were the result of something in nature that God controls (Creator). Fill out the following chart to compare the four losses.

CREATURE OR CREATOR?	DETAILS OF THE TRAGEDY	DETAILS OF JOB'S LOSS

What did Job do (a practice common in ancient cultures), after the fourth and final messenger delivered his tragic news?

⸻

If you received news of a tragic loss among your family or friends—even just one of the four kinds of tragedy Job experienced—what would be your immediate outward response (think about it through the culture and experience of your family and community)?

⸻

After Job expressed his immediate grief and sorrow for what he had lost on that day, he did something which, if we are honest, might surprise us but also challenge us to think about what we would have done in a similar situation:

> **Then he fell to the ground in worship and said:**
> **"Naked I came from my mother's womb,**
>   **and naked I will depart.**
> **The Lord gave and the Lord has taken away;**
>   **may the name of the Lord be praised."**
> **In all this, Job did not sin by charging God with wrongdoing. (Job 1:20-22)**

Job fell to the ground in worship! Think about that. He fell to the ground to say to the Lord, "You're worth it."

What is worship? Let's dig deeper into the original Hebrew word translated here as "worship." The Hebrew word occurs 172 time in the Old Testament. About 100 times it is translated as "worship," and another 50 times as "bow" or "bow down" when the context is about bowing down before other people, like a king. When the context is about bowing down before the Lord, it's translated as "worship." Worship is acknowledging that the Lord is great; that he is worthy of praise and honor; that he is so good, loving, and patient. That was Job's response after he lamented his loss—he fell to the ground in worship.

In the words that Job spoke, what was he acknowledging about himself and about the Lord?

What would have been your response after losing all your children, your employees, and all your possessions on the same day?

When tragic loss occurs, people respond in a variety of ways. What are some of the other ways people respond to loss that stand in sharp contrast to Job's response?

To accuse the Lord of wrongdoing is sin. To blame the Lord for any loss we experience is sin. So why is it so difficult for us NOT to blame God?

————

Pastor Mike mentioned the key thing that Job learned from his suffering. He said committing to this same key thing could keep us from accusing God of wrongdoing.

What was that key idea?

Are you willing to commit to it?

————

What is the most significant takeaway from chapter 2 for you?

- CHAPTER 3 -
GOD, NOT AGAIN!

PASTOR MICHAEL EWART

Let's take a look at a question that can be really challenging. Things in life get hard, suffering comes, and then it gets even worse. So the question is simply this: How do you deal when things go from bad to worse?

That happens fairly often in life, doesn't it? Something bad happens, followed by another bad thing. Oftentimes, doesn't it seem like there's usually a third bad thing too? Bad thing after bad thing after bad thing. How can your faith stand up at a time like that? What do you do when life punches you in the gut, knocks you to the ground, stomps on you, and then picks you up and body slams you again? How do you deal with that?

What is your story of when things went from bad to worse and maybe even worse yet? My aunt is going through one of those times right now. A little over a year ago, she was diagnosed with later stage leukemia. It's been a rough year for her. She had a bone marrow transplant, which is not an easy road. And then when she finally got to go home, she was in her driveway, trying to move a dumpster that was in the way. It rolled off an edge of the driveway, and she was trying to pull it back on. The dumpster tipped over onto her, and she broke her hip. She had surgery on her hip and is, once again, laid up. In a time like that, wouldn't you be tempted to say, "Seriously, God?"

Maybe you remember that Pastor Mike wrote that his life has been relatively easy. I'd have to confess the same. I haven't had an enormous amount of suffering in my 52 years of life. But I do want to share with you one story where things went from bad to worse to worse yet.

My first 12 years in the ministry were spent as a missionary in Russia. My family and I were in the middle of Russia in Siberia, not far from a city called Novosibirsk. We had been there 11 years. It was 2006, and we were traveling back to America for a furlough. We planned to be in the States for about four weeks, doing some preaching, telling people about the mission in Novosibirsk, and seeing some family and friends. We were really looking forward to that vacation back in the States.

Under normal conditions, the trip was an extraordinarily difficult and stressful trip. There were seven of us traveling; we had five children at the time. God has since blessed us with one more. So five children were making this trip with us, a trip that was about 36 hours long. These children were ages 10, 8, 5, 3, and a baby about a month and a half old. This string of kids had to help and haul their own luggage. The baby didn't have to; we gave her some slack for that first year.

It was an hour to the airport. From the airport, it was a four-and-a-half-hour flight from Novosibirsk to Moscow. From Moscow, it was a three-and-a-half-hour layover and then a trip to London. In London, there was a short overnight—seven or eight hours—not enough to get a hotel and sleep much. And from there, it was an overseas flight to Chicago where we would rent a car and drive two and a half more hours to our final destination. That's what we had to look forward to. We were stressed; we weren't really looking forward to it. We were just looking forward to getting to the States.

When we got to Moscow, we went to the British Airline check-in counter, and they looked at our documents. They said, "You might have a problem." You see, in order to get into or leave Russia, you need two documents—your U.S. passport and a Russian visa. As they looked through the documents, they found that two of our children had passports and visas that didn't match up right.

We went to passport control, knowing there might be an issue, and put the stack of seven passports and visas on the counter. I purposely put the bad two on the bottom. The worker went through them and caught the issue. She reached under the counter, flipped a switch, a red light went on above the counter, and we were ushered into a side room where no amount of pleading or explaining would change the situation. Eventually, we were told, "You are not flying out until this visa issue gets fixed."

"Okay, is there a place in the airport we can do that?"

"Well, there is a visa office; they might be able to give you some guidance."

We went there, but it was already closed because it was 7 P.M. We couldn't fly out, so we needed a place to stay. We went to an airport counter where there was a very nice, fancy hotel for $225 a night. We were poor missionaries and didn't want to pay that. So while we were standing there wrestling with this amount, a kind, old Russian babushka walked up, a nice old lady, who said, "You know what? I've got an apartment near here, and it's just ten minutes away. You can stay there for the night; I only charge $80." Done!

Forty-five minutes later, we arrived at her apartment after taking a public transportation bus, hauling all our stuff, walking through some streets, and getting to her second-floor apartment, which was an absolute dump. There were holes in the floor, no toilet seat in the bathroom, and plenty of cigarette butts everywhere. The whole place reeked. There was evidence that mice had been in there, and there was one smallish bed. We found all the bedding we could find and laid out four children across the cleanest part of the floor we could find.

I prayed there were no cockroaches or mice, and then my wife and little baby and I crowded on to the little bed and tried to sleep. My eyes were wide open as I thought about how to get out of this situation. I was careful not to roll over on the baby next to me. That's how the whole night went as we shooed away mosquitos because the screenless windows had been left open.

The next morning we decided to go to the U.S. Embassy. Surely they would help us. We took a Russian marshrutka, which is a 15-passenger van, to a bus, which took us to the underground subway called the Metro, and then we walked. An hour later, we found our way to the U.S. Embassy. We explained our problem. It was about 9:30 A.M., and we hoped we could fly out sometime that day. The embassy people said the problem was a Russian issue but offered to call them and figure things out.

We were told it could take some time, so we decided to do a little sightseeing. I called the embassy periodically to check on progress. At closing time, we were told: "Well, we did get through to them. They said they're not going to help, and there's nothing more we can do for you."

"What am I supposed to do now?" I said.

"I guess you have to go to the Russian visa office yourself and try to iron things out directly with the Russian government."

That wasn't a very good option because foreigners don't deal directly with the Russian visa office; you have a representative that does that. I wasn't sure how that was going to work. I had no idea where in this city of millions of people that office might be or how we would get there. But I did know that it was close to evening. Once again, we didn't have a place to stay. We weren't going back to that lady's apartment and had no idea how to find it anyway if we wanted to.

We remembered that there is a place in Moscow from the 1980 Olympics called Izmaylovo. It was built with thousands of hotel rooms; there were always rooms to rent there. So we took the 45-minute public transportation out to that area. We got to Hotel Alpha and went to the front counter, put down the stack of seven passports because that's how they sign people in there, and then the seven of us crashed on some couches.

As we were resting, the lady at the counter called me over. "I'm sorry, but we cannot check you into our hotel."

"What's the problem?"

"Well, you don't have an immigration card."

When you enter Russia, they give you an immigration card. I don't know what it does, but you're supposed to have it. When you exit the country, they take your immigration card. But when we were trying to exit the country the day before, they took our immigration cards and did not return them. She said, "Without that immigration card, we cannot legally register you in our hotel. And if we get checked, we will lose our license. We are not willing to take that risk, and there is no hotel in Moscow that will."

This was when I hit rock bottom. Absolutely exhausted, our family had no place to spend the night. There was no place in Moscow that would take us. I thought we could go to the main train station and just find a bench. We'd be homeless that night and sleep on a bench somewhere in Moscow. It was the most hopeless feeling I've ever had in my life as things went from bad to worse to worse yet. I didn't know what our next steps would be in the morning.

Now I'm going to leave you on that cliffhanger; I'll finish the story later. But isn't life like that sometimes? You may not have experienced something quite like that, but your struggle is no less, and it might be much longer or might involve a whole lot more pain than ours did. What do you do when things go from bad to worse to maybe even worse yet? To answer that question, we're going to turn back to the book of Job.

In the last two chapters, you read about the conversation in heaven and the challenge from Satan—"If you take away what Job has, he's not going to love you anymore." Job lost everything he had. Somebody did some modern calculations, and the value of all Job's animals plus the land that would have been needed to take care of so many animals was estimated at $60 million. And if he was using those camels for trade, he could have had a net worth of more than $100 million. He found out his net worth was knocked down to zero in one day, but that wasn't the worst of it. The same day a wind blew down a house where his ten children were, and they died. And Job said, **"The Lord gave and the Lord has taken away; may the name of the Lord be praised"** (Job 1:21). He fell down and worshiped the Lord.

Except there are 41 more chapters to the book of Job. So we're going to look at a few verses from chapter 2 because we're going to find out that Satan wasn't done.

Even though things looked about as bad as they could possibly get for Job, they weren't. Satan wasn't done yet, and there was one more tremendous challenge in front of Job.

"On another day the angels came to present themselves before the Lord, **and Satan also came with them to present himself before him. The** Lord **said to Satan, 'Where have you come from?' Satan answered the** Lord, **'From roaming throughout the earth, going back and forth on it'"** (2:1,2). So again, we have this mysterious situation where God meets with angels and demons. I wish I could tell you more about what that's all about or how often that happens, but we don't have a ton of information in the Bible about that.

"Then the Lord **said to Satan, 'Have you considered my servant, Job? There is no one on earth like him; he is blameless and upright, a man who fears God and shuns evil. And he still maintains his integrity, though you incited me against him to ruin him without any reason'"** (verse 3). And if any of this sounds familiar, it's because that's what we were reading about in Job chapter 1. Satan appeared. God bragged on Job and said, "Have you seen such a faithful man in all your life?" Satan said, "Well, of course he's faithful. You've given him so much stuff. He loves the stuff you give, not you. Take away the stuff, and he won't love you anymore." God said, "Challenge accepted."

Satan took everything, and Job remained faithful and

worshiped the Lord. So God said, "Did you notice? You lost! He's still faithful to me. He still loves me. He still knows I love him. Satan, you lost." If Satan were reasonable, which he's not, he would have licked his wounds, cowered away with his tail between his legs, and never shown up in the Lord's presence again. But Satan is not rational; he's vicious. And he said, "Well, of course he still loves you; he still has his health. If you take that away, he will curse you."

"'Skin for skin!' Satan replied. 'A man will give all he has for his own life. But now stretch out your hand and strike his flesh and bones, and he will surely curse you to your face.' The Lord said to Satan, 'Very well, then, he is in your hands; but you must spare his life'" (verses 4–6). So once again, God gave free rein (to a point) to Satan to do his worst, and I want you to notice here what Satan did. In both of these circumstances, God said, "Okay. You can go this far, but no farther." And how far did Satan go? Absolutely as far as he possibly could. He hates us so much and God so much that he will take every inch of what God gives him, every last millimeter of it. He will go to the limit of what God allows in order to bring harm and suffering upon God's people.

"So Satan went out from the presence of the Lord and afflicted Job with painful sores from the soles of his feet to the crown of his head. Then Job took a piece of broken pottery and scraped himself with it as he sat among the ashes" (verses 7,8). From head to toe, Job had extraordinarily painful boils that itched and hurt. He found no relief from them. Finally, a broken piece of pottery gave him the only little bit of relief he could find. It was a horrible illness. I don't know what it was in modern terms or if we have enough details to say exactly what his ailment was, but it was horrible.

If you look through the rest of Job, you can find a few more details about the nature of Job's illness. There was insomnia; he had an incredibly difficult time sleeping. There were worms that crawled in his flesh. He had nightmares and horrible bad breath. Weight loss. Chills, which means there was probably bad fevers. Diarrhea is hinted at in one verse. His skin was turning black, called necrosis, probably because some of it was dying. He was so horribly disfigured that when his friends finally came and visited him, they were struck silent at his appearance for seven days straight. They couldn't find a word to speak. Job's appearance was so horrific that all they could do was sit and stare.

That is what Job was dealing with. It was extraordinarily personal; his own body was afflicted. If you've ever experienced pain, especially for extended periods of time or especially pain that hits 10 on the 1 to 10 scale, you know how hard that can be. Pain removes perspective, it stops you from thinking clearly, it shortens your vision, and you can't think much beyond what you're feeling in that moment. And that's where Job was as all his health was taken away.

And then this: **"His wife said to him, 'Are you still maintaining your integrity? Curse God and die!'"** (verse 9). Well, that's helpful. His wife wasn't much support. Some people jokingly say there's a reason that Satan didn't take Job's wife from him; she was part of the suffering. But you know what, to be perfectly honest, I don't think we should be too hard on her. This was a woman who had suffered like Job had. She too had gone from riches to rags.

GOD GETS TO CALL THE SHOTS.

This woman, this mother of ten, became a mother of none in one moment. Her head was reeling too. She was hurting; she was suffering.

Now I think she understood a couple of things about God but not a third thing, and I'm going to share all three of those with you shortly. But look at Job's reaction. Job replied: **"'You are talking like a foolish woman. Shall we accept good from God and not trouble?' In all this, Job did not sin in what he said"** (verse 10).

Job still didn't sin against God. He understood that God gets to call the shots. God brought good, and now God brought trouble. Either way, we just have to accept whatever God gives; that was Job's conclusion, which is incredible. How could Job still worship God, still trust God, in a time like this? The answer is simply this—it has to be this—Job was prepared for the pain, and that's one of the first takeaways I want you to remember: *Prepare before the pain.* Because here's the truth: When the pain comes, when the stress comes, when things go from bad to worse to worse, you are not thinking as rationally as you are right now. You are not a good student in that moment. The time for you to learn how a parachute works is not after you jump out of the airplane.

My son did a tandem jump out of an airplane last summer. He spent at least half an hour, maybe a little bit more, learning how it was going to work: what to do, when to pull the ripcord, how to move, when to jump. He did that all before they jumped, not during. And before is the time for us to prepare for pain. If you're not in pain now, you've got some work to do because now is the time to prepare.

How do you and I prepare? We prepare by listening to God. Jesus himself told us how important it is to prepare in Matthew chapter 7. This was right after he taught the Sermon on the Mount for three chapters straight: **"Therefore everyone who hears these words of mine and puts them into practice** [whoever knows what I just taught and does it, whoever believes in it and lives it] **is like a wise man who built his house on the rock. The rain came down, the streams rose, and the winds blew and beat against that house; yet it did not fall, because it had its foundation on the rock"** (verses 24,25). Does that remind you of Job? There was a horrible storm in his life and then another storm and another storm, and he did not fall. He did not collapse. Jesus said, **"But everyone who hears these words of mine and does not put** them into practice is like a foolish man who built his house on sand. The rain came down, the streams rose, and the winds blew and beat against that house, and it fell with a great crash" (verses 26,27). The person who isn't prepared for the storms of life sees his or her life come down with a crash.

So how did Job prepare? We're left to guess a little bit here because we don't have a lot of the details. We do know that Job was prepared. He was already worshiping God. He already knew what kind of God he had. When his children had a party, he thought maybe one of them sinned. He didn't know that they did, but maybe in their partying, somebody said something stupid, somebody got drunk, maybe somebody did something wrong. So **GOD IS SOVEREIGN.** after anytime there was a party, he offered a sacrifice to God to ask him to forgive his children. Doesn't that show us that Job had prepared? He knew that God is a God of justice and also a God of love who forgives.

Job, in his preparation for the pain, knew two things about God: He knew that God is transcendent and that God is sovereign. Those are two words we don't use a lot, right? *Transcendent* means that God is awesome; God is an awesome God, and he reigns in the heavens above. He is transcendent, beyond us. And he is sovereign; God is absolutely independent. God gets to make all the choices. God doesn't owe us an explanation for any of his choices because God is sovereign.

Those two words are a little bit hard to remember, especially if you haven't heard their definitions before, so let me give you a more simplified and memorable definition. What is true about God? God is large—and you might guess what's next—and in charge! That means that God is transcendent and God is sovereign. God is awesome. He is incredible. He is amazing. He is beyond understanding. He is beyond time. He is beyond space. He is wise beyond our greatest imaginings. God is large, and so we magnify him. We worship him. We praise him because God is powerful and in charge. In charge means he controls all things. In Psalm 115:3, we read this, **"Our God is in heaven; he does whatever pleases him."** What does God do? Whatever he wants. Who does he have to check with? Nobody. He is God, and he is in charge. He is in heaven; he does whatever pleases him. And this is what led Job to say, "Shall we accept good from God, and not trouble?" We've got to accept both because God is large and God is in charge.

Now here is where I would suggest that Job's wife believed the same thing about God. She knew God is large and in charge and there's nothing we can do about it. She said, "He gets to call the shots; that's why you need to curse God and die, Job, because look at how he's treating you. There's no recourse for you. There's nothing you can do about it, so you might as well curse him and die. He's obviously against you." God is large and in charge, and that fact alone did not create faith in her heart or give her any sort of encouragement or hope. And yet, that is the first thing we must understand about God. It's the first thing we must do in order to prepare for the pain: to know the truth that God is the one in charge.

But that's not enough. There's a third thing you need to know about God that is even more important. Without this third thing, the first two things are terrifying. The third thing is this: *God is love.* If God is large and in charge but he hates you or doesn't know you or could care less about you or has it in for you, curse God and die. But if God is large and in charge and loves you, well, that's a different story. That means even if there's trouble coming into your life, there must be a reason because God is good and God is love.

How can we be sure that's true? How do we know that all the bad could still work out for good? God himself promises it: **"We know that in all things God works for the good of those who love him"** (Romans 8:28). In *all* things. Not in some things, not occasionally in things, but in all things God works for good. He *always* works for the good of those who love him, for those who have been called according to his purpose.

And then the apostle Paul says these words of comfort: **"Who shall separate us from the love of Christ? Shall trouble or hardship or persecution or famine or nakedness or danger or sword?"** (Romans 8:35). Losing your entire net worth? or your children? or your health? Will those separate you from the love of Christ? Will persecution or famine or nakedness or danger or sword separate you? There's a violent war going on in your neighborhood; would that separate you from the love of Christ? The conclusion: No. **"In all these things we are more than conquerors through him who loved us"** (verse 37). And then Paul says this: **"For I am convinced that neither death nor life, neither angels nor demons, neither the present nor the future, nor any powers, neither height nor depth, nor anything else in all creation, will be able to separate us from the love of God that is in Christ Jesus our Lord"** (verses 38,39). Nothing that can happen in this world will ever separate you from the love of God—and this is key—that is in Christ Jesus our Lord. How can you know for a fact that God loves you and that he's for you and that he's with you and that he really will work this all out for blessing? Because he did not hold back what was nearest and dearest to him but gave him up for you, namely, his Son, Jesus.

Jesus came and took on human flesh knowing it would mean pain and knowing he would suffer. He said, "Sign me up because I love them." He was perfect for us. He took the blame for us for all our sin. He took it to the cross and paid our sin debt in full. He did this at the highest cost to himself imaginable, giving his life for us. He did this at the highest amount of pain we can possibly imagine—not just the physical pain, which was horrendous—but the spiritual pain of being separated from the heavenly Father. His Father turned his back on his Son because our sin, our filth, our guilt was all on him. The Father said, "I cannot look," and Jesus cried out, "My God, my God, why have you forsaken me?" Because of us, that's why.

Jesus could cry out from the cross at the end, "It is finished." Our sin was paid for. The Father accepted this payment, and you and I are not guilty. **"He was delivered over to death for our sins and was raised to life for our justification"** (Romans 4:25). Nothing can separate us from that love that is ours in Christ Jesus. God will work everything for good; it's his promise.

He did for me and my family when we were stuck in Moscow back in 2006. Things took a turn for the better after that very low moment. While we were stressing out, trying to figure out our next steps, somebody back in Novosibirsk was helping us get our visa thing straightened out, pulling some strings, and greasing some wheels. I didn't ask too many questions. The visas were delivered to us. We then found out that the British Airlines was backed up because somebody had tried to blow up a plane with gel in their shoes. Because of the backup, we were stuck in Moscow for six more days.

But it was good! We had one of the best, most memorable family vacations of a lifetime. We stayed in a tiny hotel room, used the Metro to see the city. We saw Red Square, the Kremlin, a 3-D movie, and a couple museums. God turned it out for good. Was it enormously stressful? Yes. Was it the path I would have chosen? Absolutely not, but in the end, we have some incredible family memories. The Lord took what was to us bad and stressful and turned it into a blessing, because that's what God does.

Now the truth is, you might be reading this story and thinking, "Really? That's the worst thing you could come up with? My pain has been going on for years. My struggle has been a lifetime. I have suffered far worse than anything you just mentioned." But God's truth is unchanged, and I want you to remember this: *Nothing will be able to separate you from the love of God that is in Christ Jesus our Lord.*

There's a member of our church who said I could share her story; I'll have to greatly abbreviate it. Her name is Kaz, and she went through so much in her life. Here are a few things that she shared. By the age of six, she had endured every type of abuse. Her mother struggled with alcoholism, and her stepfather was abusive. She became the primary caregiver for her younger siblings at a very young age, and at the age of 14, the entire family ended up homeless. Her faith hung on by a thread because things kept going from bad to worse to worse yet. Yet nothing separated her from the love of God in Christ Jesus.

God brought her through that and shaped the circumstances of her life to draw her back close to him again. She was so overjoyed to find out about our church and to get to know Jesus even better through it that she said this: "I can't describe how my salvation has felt in words. I imagine a dirty, poor little girl dressed in rags with no family, lost in a crowd. Jesus parts the crowd to reach her. He picks her up and says, 'She's mine!' He cleanses her with Baptism, removing the dirt. He dresses her in his armor, protecting her from danger. He feeds her with his words and wisdom. And when she's standing in front of the mirror amazed by the difference, he tells her he is going to pay all her fines. All

GOD IS LARGE AND IN CHARGE.

the times she stole to eat, lied to survive, disregarded the rules—she is no longer responsible for it. The verdict was death, but he loved her so much he would die in her place. He decided this, even when she was dirty, poor, and in rags." Kaz said, "I feel like that little girl."

Kaz wasn't prepared for the pain, but she sure is now. She knows, and you know too. God is large and in charge, and he loves you more than you can possibly imagine. He loves you. Job believed that. Kaz believes it. I pray you do too.

PRAYER

Heavenly Father, there is so much ugliness in this broken world and so much pain and suffering. It's not unusual for people, including people who call themselves Christians, to go from bad to worse to worse yet. So help me prepare, to set my eyes on you, to recognize that you are the awesome eternal God and that you are in charge of all things. You are transcendent and sovereign. But never let me take my eyes off the cross, the proof and the guarantee of your love for me. Help me believe and rejoice in the fact that nothing will ever separate me from your love that is in Christ Jesus my Lord. In him I am forgiven, in him I am your child, and in him I am cleansed. I am yours, and I praise your holy name.

Give me the strength, Lord, no matter what happens in this world, to fall to the ground and worship you as my loving God. I pray this all in the powerful name of Jesus. Amen.

FOR FURTHER STUDY: GOD, NOT AGAIN!

DR. BRUCE BECKER

In chapter 3, Pastor Michael Ewart referenced how it seems that bad things happen in clusters of two or three or more. That was my understanding growing up as a kid. I learned that idea from the adults in my life. It seemed that among my extended family, there was this sense of bad things happening to people in "groups of three."

What's been your experience when it comes to bad things happening in clusters?

Do you have any personal examples to share from your life where one bad thing was followed by another bad thing and maybe even a third bad thing?

In Job chapter 2, Satan is back in the Lord's presence along with the holy angels who serve the Lord. After asking Satan where he has come from, the Lord says: **"Have** you considered my **servant Job? There is no one on earth like him; he is blameless and upright, a man who fears God and shuns evil. And he still maintains his integrity, though you incited me against him to ruin him without any reason"** (verse 3).

There are three key phrases in the last sentence. They give us insight into the Lord's role in Satan's first challenge, Job's response, and Satan's goal. What are those three key phrases, and what is the significance of each?

1.

2.

3.

The Lord said that Job maintained his "integrity" throughout his tragic loss of people and possessions. Job's wife also used this word at the end of the chapter with the encouragement that Job forfeit his integrity, curse God, and die.

Let's dig a little deeper into the word *integrity*. The Hebrew word translated as "integrity" also has these other shades of meaning: "completeness," "purity," "innocence," "respectability," and "spotless character."

Based upon these various shades of meaning of the

original Hebrew word, how would you, in your own words, describe Job's integrity?

———

Satan didn't agree with the Lord's assessment of Job. Instead, he made another accusation against Job.

What was that accusation?

———

What was Satan's next challenge to the Lord involving Job?

———

The Lord agreed to Satan's challenge. But once again the Lord placed a limit on what Satan could do to Job.

What was the limitation?

———

What Satan did to Job is summarized in this chapter as **"painful sores from the soles of his feet to the crown of his head"** (Job 2:7). But there was far more Job had to endure. Look up the following passages from Job for more details of what Job endured because of these painful sores:

Job 2:12,13

Job 3:26

Job 7:5

Job 7:13,14

Job 19:17

Job 19:20

Job 30:30

———

Most people, Christian and non-Christian alike, don't go through life without some kind of pain. It can be physical pain or the pain resulting from a crippling illness. It can be the emotional pain linked to mental illness. It can be the pain caused by strained and broken relationships. It can be the pain of financial loss or just struggling each day to make ends meet.

Consider for yourself or share with others in your group the worst pain you've ever experienced, how you dealt with it, and whether it is still a reality or is now in your past.

Pastor Michael talked about "preparing for pain." He contrasted Job, who apparently was prepared for pain, with his wife, who wasn't prepared for her or her husband's pain at all. Their conversation is insightful: **"His wife said to him, 'Are you still maintaining your integrity? Curse God and die!' He replied, 'You are talking like a foolish woman. Shall we accept good from God,**

and not trouble?' In all this, Job did not sin in what he said" (Job 2:9,10).

Pastor Michael mentioned several ways we can prepare for pain so that when we experience it, we can respond like Job. List the various ways Pastor Michael said we can prepare for pain. Add to the list any additional thoughts that you have:

-

-

-

-

-

What is the most significant takeaway from chapter 3 for you?

- CHAPTER 4 -

HOW AM I SUPPOSED TO COMFORT OTHERS?

I couldn't wait to ask the pastors from my church just one question. The five of us had gathered around a conference room table to discuss an up-and-coming sermon series, like we always did, and this time the series we were discussing was a series on the book of Job. It was a series about pain and suffering, about the hard times we go through in life, and how we deal with it together. And the question I couldn't wait to ask the other pastors was this: What do you guys do? When someone from our church whose life has gone from good to not so good to really, really bad, what do you do? When someone pours out their heart, when the tears start to fall, what do you do? What do you say? When you grab your Bible, what page do you turn to? How do you try to help people who are hurting?

One of the really cool and really humbling parts of what we do is that people tend to come to us, to the church and to pastors, when times are really, really good or when they're really, really not. "We conceived, we're going to have a baby, and we're going to start a family.

Let's tell the pastor, and let's pray about that." Or when they can't have kids or when there's been a miscarriage, people tell the pastors about that. When a relationship has gone from something special to thinking about marriage, people call the pastor. Or when things get really bad and someone drops the "D" word—there's a separation or a divorce—they call the pastor. When there's a celebration, they call the pastor. When it's cancer, they call the pastor. We get to ride the roller coaster of the ups and downs of life.

So I wanted to ask these guys this: When it's not the ups but it's the downs, what do you do? I'm a guy who's pretty good at the ups and the Bible passages about joy. It's just how I'm wired. I'll quote *Dumb & Dumber* or *Anchorman*, and we'll have a good time together. But when it dips, I feel incompetent emotionally. What do you say? I know the Bible; I could come up with an intellectual, good, biblical answer that applies, but that's not always how you help people, right? It's about the emotional IQ, knowing what to say, how to say it, and how often to say it. And so, I asked the pastors: What do you do?

I can ask you the same question: What do you do? You don't have to be a trained pastor in theology to walk with someone in one of these moments of life. When one of your friends or the girl you're dating or your mom or your dad or your roommates come to you with the breakup, with Grandpa's death, with the cancer, with the miscarriage, what do you do?

It happens to all of us, right? Life in this world is filled with joys and sorrows, and if we don't live in a cave by ourselves, it involves doing life with people and their joys and their sorrows. If you're a person of faith, what do you say about God and Jesus and the Bible? What chapter and verse do you turn to? What do you do in the midst of brokenness and pain?

THIS WORLD IS FILLED WITH JOYS AND SORROWS.

I was trying to think through my own experience with conversations like that. What have I tended to do? What sometimes works? I came up with my own top 10 list. So here are the top 10 things I think people like us do when people we love are dealing with pain.

1. *Just be there.* You don't have to quote the prophet Isaiah. Sometimes when you show up and give someone a hug, you're physically present. It's a great gift not to go through tough moments alone. You could just be there.

2. *Say sorry.* "I'm so sorry you're going through this. When I heard the news, I was devastated. I can't believe this happened." That emotion is technically what sympathy is. In Greek, the word *pathy* means "emotion or suffering"; *sym* means "with or together." When you line up your emotion with theirs, it feels so good to go through that together.

3. *Share a story.* "I don't think I ever told you this, but did you know my grandpa died when I was your age?" "The whole world doesn't know this, but I actually went

through two miscarriages too; I know what that feels like." When people realize they're not the first to go through it and somehow you've gotten through it, it gives them hope for the future.

4. *Offer help.* Have you ever heard of the casserole crew after a funeral? We don't know what to do, so we make food; we drop it off on the doorstep. "Can I watch the kids and give you a day to yourself?" "Can I clean the house?"

5. *Offer hope.* You could say, "I know right now this feels like it's never ever going to get better, but time will heal wounds. I used to be where you are, and God got me through it. I've learned great lessons from it. This isn't the end of the story. This feeling won't endure forever."

6. *Offer a bit of silver lining.* "It's bad, but there's still something good. You could grumble about what you've lost, but there's really something even in this moment to be grateful for." I sometimes say this when I'm at a funeral and it's a packed church. I say, "Man, I'm so sorry for your loss, but this is incredible. Your dad was so loved." "Your grandma impacted so many." Look around and see the value and the impact that this life made.

7. *Preach about God's plans.* God has a plan for this. It's painful, but for Christians, pain is never pointless. The devil loves to take away, and God loves to flip it for the good of his people. There are passages like these: **"I know the plans I have for you"** (Jeremiah 29:11). **"In all things God works for the good of those who love him"** (Romans 8:28). The whole universe is underneath the

feet of Jesus (Ephesians 1). "God is going to use this. You can't see it, and I don't know exactly why, but God has promised it is never, ever, ever pointless."

8. My favorite—*you could preach GOD's presence*. GOD! Leave the caps lock on. GOD! The best thing about our lives is that he is still present. "You lost a baby, but you did not lose God." "Your husband walked out the door, but Jesus is a better husband and will never leave or forsake his church." "Your friend disappointed you, betrayed you, moved to the other side of the country. Jesus is the friend who said, 'I will be with you always.'" You might lose many things in this life, but if you are a Christian, there is one thing you never, ever, ever, ever have to wonder about losing: It's the presence of a loving and glorious God.

9. *Preach God's sympathy*. There are some interesting passages in the book of Hebrews that say because Jesus was human, because he walked among us on this very same planet for 33 years, he knows what it's like. Has the system failed you? Jesus knows. Have you lost someone you care about? Jesus knows. Have you wept? Jesus did. Have you been betrayed? Jesus was too. Are you in physical pain? Jesus was too. Has the church disappointed you? It disappointed Jesus too. Has your family disappointed you? Jesus too. When you pray to Jesus about your pain, he nods because he knows. He knows exactly what it's like to feel how you feel because he felt it first.

10. *Preach God's salvation*. You could tell your loved

one, "Hey, listen, because of Jesus, the story will not end this way. Eternity is like a thousand-foot rope, and the Bible says the pain you're going through is like one little inch of black tape on that rope. It's hard now, and it might not get better tomorrow, but the Bible says Jesus is coming back to save his people from sorrow and death and mourning and grief and pain. We are forgiven now, and we will not have to struggle forever."

What do you think about my list? As you look it over, circle one of the things that you default to when you're face-to-face with pain. Or are there two or three options on your roadmap for helping people who are suffering? As you think about that though, I want to suggest one complicating factor: Many of the things on my list can backfire. Have you noticed that? It's a good thing on paper, but depending on whom you're talking to and what their emotional state is in the moment, something that might be really good for one person is really, really not so good for another person, right? Maybe a yellow flag in your brain went up when I suggested, "Offer a silver lining." "Hey, your husband's dead, but look at all the people at his funeral; isn't that great?" That can backfire; that can be really insensitive. Sometimes saying God has a plan for you can backfire. You know, a person is empty; they've lost a child or the closest person they loved is gone. "God has plans!" And someone might lash out and say, "What kind of God is this that would have plans to make me feel like that? If I'm his child, why would he let that happen?"

You could try to share your story, and someone could throw that back at you: "You don't know what I'm going through. You did that, but this is so much worse."

I've realized over time that it's complicated and messy, and there's no perfect script and no page in the Bible that says, "Step one, say this. Step two, do that." So there's this tension, isn't there? We all end up in these conversations with people who are feeling incredible pain. We want to do something good and helpful, and very few of us know exactly what that helpful thing to do is.

That's why I'm excited to share just three little verses from the end of Job chapter 2, because this tension that we feel, it's not the first time. Many, many years ago, Job's life went from good to bad to unthinkably bad. And at the very end of Job chapter 2, his friends show up. They try to deal with this situation that we all deal with. They're good friends; they care about Job. What will they do? What will they say? Let's take a peek at what these friends did and then think about what we can do for each other when moments like this turn into moments like that.

Job 2:11: **"When Job's three friends, Eliphaz the Temanite, Bildad the Shuhite and Zophar the Naamathite, heard about all the troubles that had come upon him, they set out from their homes and met together by agreement to go and sympathize with him and comfort him."**

Let's pause there. Based on that one verse, these are amazing friends, right? This isn't like Facebook friends.

Think for a second about what these guys did. It says, "When they heard about Job's troubles, they set out from their homes." This implies that they left their families, their friends, their jobs, their to-do lists, their beds, their comfort and traveled to see Job. We're going to find out that they will spend more than a week of personal time off to try to be a friend to their broken friend named Job. These are ride-or-die, stand-up-next-to-you-at-your-wedding, carry-the-casket-at-your-funeral kind of friends. They care so much about Job. The text says they "met together by agreement." They said, "We've got to do something. What are we going to do? I don't know, but let's get together; let's brainstorm. Let's come up with some plan because Job is at the bottom, and he needs us right now." Job didn't invite them; he didn't say, "You guys have got to come." They just knew because this is what great friends do; Job needed help.

According to the same verse, when they met together by agreement, they came up with three goals. First of all, their goal was to go. Goal number two was to sympathize, and goal number three was to comfort. They said, "We've got to go." Sometimes sending a text, a Snapchat message, writing a letter, or calling with Facetime works, but sometimes you've got to go. Sometimes you're close enough to that person and the relationship is there where you just physically have to be at the funeral. A digital hug is nice; an actual hug is about a thousand times better.

Next they said they needed to sympathize with Job.

The Hebrew word used here for *sympathize* literally means "to do this; to move to and fro." It's like when someone shares terrible news with you and your heart shakes your head, "No, oh, man." They said, "We've got to show Job this is so bad, this is not the way that life is supposed to be. We want to sympathize with him; we want to mirror his emotions."

And then finally, they said, "We want to go comfort him." They couldn't bring back Job's deceased children, they couldn't cure all his illnesses, but somehow they wanted to say something or do something to make it just one percent more comfortable. Let's go, let's sympathize, let's comfort him; those were the three goals of these three incredible friends.

It makes me think of some of my friends. About a month ago, I was at a middle-school volleyball game and one of my classmates, who's a pastor here in our town, said, "Did you hear about Nate?" I had no clue, but I found out that one of our classmates, a 40-year-old pastor in Kansas, had died of COVID. Just like that, gone. Married not that long ago. Four kids ages 7 and under. And I can't imagine his wife waking up with four kids needing attention. But then I heard what some of his friends did. Nate was blessed with a lot of friends—I was maybe in his second circle—but his inner circle, the guys he had known long before he met me, did exactly what Job's friends did. They met together digitally and said, "What are we going to do? We've got to go." These pastors left behind churches and families and children and jobs. They took personal time off, piled into a couple cars in Wisconsin, and drove 600 miles to Kansas just to go and to sympathize and to comfort. They hugged the recent widow. They spoke words of grace in Jesus to these little kids. They actually formed a choir and stood up and sang about God's glory and the beauty of heaven at this man's funeral. They couldn't fix it, they couldn't bring Nate back, but they were friends. And this is what friends do. They physically go, they emotionally sympathize, and they verbally comfort.

So let me ask you: Is there someone in your life right now who needs you to do the same thing? I'm choosing that word carefully—*needs*. Every weekend in my planning journal, I write myself a question: Mike, who needs a pastor? Sometimes a pastor's nice, "Hey, let's catch up. Let's grab some coffee. Would you pray for me? Can you answer this question about the Bible?" Sometimes that's nice, but sometimes you just need it, right? It's as bad as life has been in a long time. So let me ask you that question: Who needs you right now? If you took five seconds right now, could you think of a friend, a family member, a neighbor who's maybe dealing with one of the killer Ds: disease, death, divorce, or depression?

Here's the deal: They need you. They might not have the words to tell you, they might be embarrassed to ask you, but when people hit bottom, they need you. Do you know what Jesus himself said the night before he died?

He went to a garden to pray and said to his friends, "Stay with me. I'm so overwhelmed with sorrow. Stay; I need you." Your friends need you too. You might not know how to fix it. Your plan might not be perfect, but they need you. So I want to urge you; I want to push you. Just show up. Bring a casserole, send a text, give them a heads-up. It might be messy, it might be imperfect, but the fact is we need each other in moment's like that. How good and pleasant it is, the Bible says, when people live together in unity. If one person lies down alone, how sad. But where two are there together, how good, Ecclesiastes chapter 4 says.

AFTER TRAGEDY, COMMUNITY IS NECESSARY.

Brainstorm with a couple of friends; meet together by agreement; come up with your own plan to go, to sympathize, and to comfort because here is what I have learned: These are the moments in life that people remember. When people just show up, that's the stuff that sticks with us, doesn't it? People don't remember what you cooked. They probably don't remember what Bible passage you quoted. But the fact that you were there when they needed someone to be there is so important. I want to encourage you; God is telling you go, go, go; they need you.

After tragedy, community is a necessity. It's not nice; it's what we need, just like Jesus.

So what comes next? These three friends came up

with their three goals, their plan. Let's jump back into Job chapter 2 to see what happens next: **"When they [the three friends] saw him from a distance, they could hardly recognize him; they began to weep aloud, and they tore their robes and sprinkled dust on their heads. Then they sat on the ground with him for seven days and seven nights. No one said a word to him, because they saw how great his suffering was"** (verses 12,13).

Can you imagine what Job must have looked like? What state are you in when your best friends see you and don't speak a word? I was reading some Bible commentaries on this chapter, and one pastor had read through the book of Job and highlighted every physical thing that Job was dealing with. I never knew this, and I want to share the list. He said that Job's suffering included, quote, "Inflamed ulcerous sores, persistent itching, disfiguration, loss of appetite, worm-infested skin that burst open, scabbed over, cracked, oozed, and pussed, difficulty breathing, foul breath, loss of weight, high fever, chills, diarrhea, depression, anxiety and excruciating continual pain."[1] That's what they saw. And they couldn't say a word. They didn't even recognize him. So they tore their robes like Job tore his. They sprinkled dust on their heads like Job shaved his own head. And they just sat down on the ground for seven days. They didn't go back home; they didn't get a nice hotel room;

[1] Charles R. Swindoll, *Job: A Man of Heroic Endurance* (Nashville: Thomas Nelson, 2009), 33.

they just sat with their friend for seven straight days. And, "No one said a word to him because they saw how great his suffering was."

What do you think about that? Do you think the fact that Job's closest friends didn't say a word for seven days was a good way to help their hurting friend or a bad way to help their hurting friend? Some people think this is good. In fact, in Jewish culture, when you walk into the home of someone who's suffering, you don't speak first. You don't impose your conversation upon them. You wait for them to speak, and you see where they're at. What do you say when all your children are gone? What exactly do you say? God has a plan for you? No, I think it was brilliant that they just sat there with him.

If you know about the 35 chapters that come next in the book of Job, once these men open their mouths— boom—it all goes off the tracks. They try to explain why this would happen. They start to say, "Maybe, Job, you're not as good as everyone thought." The conversation explodes into the longest argument between four men that you've ever read in the Bible in your entire life. So maybe the best thing these guys could do was just sit on the ground with this broken man.

But other people, including some pretty great theologians and Bible commentators, say what the friends did wasn't so great. Imagine if you are Job. You are in a car wreck, and everyone you loved in the car is gone. You are hooked up to tubes, and I come to see you in the hospital. I see you there, and I just weep. I sit down and hold your hand. If I did that for an hour, you'd be like, "What a pastor!" If I did that for a day, you'd be like, "His hand is kind of sweaty." If I sat by your side for a week and didn't say a word, would that be awkward? I'm thinking, "Well, say something. What are you thinking?" So there's this great debate. Was this the best thing the friends ever did? Was this the most awkward, insensitive thing the friends ever did? And I actually love the fact that there's some ambiguity here, because here's the second big idea I want to share with you. After tragedy, community is messy. It just is. When people are hurting, when we walk into a conversation that is filled with pain, it's not clear cut. It's not black and white. It is so, so messy.

Do you walk into the room and say something? Maybe. Do you stick around because she's going to need so much help after the death of the one she loved? Maybe. Does she want some space and privacy to mourn? Maybe. Do you ask a question like, "Hey, if you need any help, text me, okay?" Maybe. Is asking a person who just can't think straight to come up with a list of good things to do the right thing to do? Maybe. Do you open a Bible and share your own story and testimony? Maybe. Is it the wrong time to share that? Maybe. Do you remind a person that God is powerful and is going to work this for their good just like the Bible says? Maybe. Will someone be mad at God in that moment? Maybe. When someone in their pain says something about God that's not biblically true, when they question his love and his plans, do you become like the theologian hawk? Swoop in and correct them so the lie doesn't grow in their hearts? Maybe. Do you understand that hurt people say things they don't mean? Probably. What do you do? And the Bible's answer is you try; it's messy. After tragedy, community is a necessity. We need people, but the reality is that community is also messy. Those people are going to walk in the room, and it's not going to be perfect.

So let me make two quick applications. Number one, if you are the friend today who goes to be with a friend, here's my advice to you: Expect messy. Ditch the perfectionist mindset that doesn't ever work in life but especially in these moments. Expect it to be messy. Expect that you're going to mess up. Expect that you're going to say the wrong thing at the wrong time. In fact, I think it would be brilliant if you would say to your hurting friend, "Hey, listen, I really don't know what to do. And I have a hunch I'm going to say something I don't intend, but it might happen. If that happens or when that happens, just please know that I realize I'm not perfect but I do want to be present. If I say something wrong, tell me. Please, I'll do my best to correct it, but I don't want you to go through this season of life alone." Expect it to be messy.

When you're driving home or you're holding your phone waiting for them to text back and you're beating yourself up because you feel guilty that you said this or you should have said that or you didn't say that, here's the beauty about being a Christian: There's always Jesus. There's a Jesus who died on a cross to forgive every sin, including the sins we don't intend. Jesus is the Savior whose blood cleans up the mess so that we don't have to live with guilt and think we're so stupid for saying the wrong thing when a person needed us most. Christianity says we can repent, which means we can confess our sins and then know that God always does. The rock-solid foundation that we have as we go through this is the constant love and forgiveness of Jesus Christ. So go somewhere. Help someone. Expect it to be messy, and know that Jesus always cleans up the mess.

Second, if you feel like Job, if my examples of disease or death or divorce or depression are what you're going through right now, here's my advice to you: Expect messy. I wish your friends and family were Jesus. They aren't. They're sinful people, and their sins are sometimes going to happen at the worst times.

Just after I was born, my parents had another child. The child, Jimmy, was sick; he died at just six weeks old. My mom called the pastor, and the pastor's wife picked up. Do you know the first thing she said to my mom? "Praise Jesus." Wrong answer. There's a time to praise Jesus, but there is a time not to speak. The pastor's wife messed up because she's a person. And people are going to mess up; they're going to disappoint you. You're going to wish they showed up, and they didn't. You're going to wish they would just give you some space, and they won't. You're going to wish they'd stop blowing up your phone because you just need silence. You're going to wish, as you stare at your phone, that someone would reach out, and they won't. They can't read hearts or minds; but know this: It is infinitely better to go through pain with messy friends than with no friends at all. So don't let the devil dupe you. Don't hold it against them and let that seed of bitterness take root. Don't replay the conversation and punish them again and again. If you have to talk to them about it, talk to them and then extend to them the same forgiveness and grace that God has extended to you.

That's the beauty about being a Christian. We've received so much forgiveness from Jesus. He forgives and forgives and forgives and forgives, and that's so good for us. It prepares us to extend that forgiveness to those who mess up. Thank God that they showed up. Forgive them for their sins, and don't let the devil mess with the community that is a necessity after our tragedies.

So what are you going to do? Who's the person? What's the step? What's the forgiveness? Here's what I'm super grateful for: In this broken world, you and I are not alone.

That's what Mike told me. Mike is a member of our church who leads a local chapter of a program called Grief Share. This is a small group for people who have lost those whom they dearly loved. I knew Mike had infinitely more experience than I did in this area, so I asked him the simple question by email. I said, "Mike, does community really make a difference? When you're in that spot of deep grief, does this matter or am I just reading too much into this?" He responded, "Pastor Mike, we will all grieve differently and for different lengths of time. However, there are two things in common to all. We cannot do this alone. And above all, we cannot do this without God." You cannot do this alone. And you can't do it without God. Because of Jesus and our community, we don't have to.

So when you have those highs and lows, expect them to be messy and thank God for Jesus.

PRAYER

Heavenly Father, I pray for patience. The Bible says that the only reason you haven't come back yet to end this brokenness is because you love people who are not believers just yet— people who still have doubts, people who question you, people who don't believe that you died for the forgiveness of their sins. They matter so much to you, God, that you're still waiting. So I pray for patience. Help me love and serve others well in the moments until you come back. Then there will be no more mourning and no more crying and no more death and no more divorce and no more depression. Brokenness will be gone, the old ways will be passed, and the new will come. I ache for that day. I know you're going to get me there. So inspire me, God. Forgive me. Lead me as I race to the finish line where I'll see your face and where pain is gone forever. I pray this all with confidence because of your glorious Son. Amen.

FOR FURTHER STUDY:
HOW AM I SUPPOSED TO COMFORT OTHERS?
DR. BRUCE BECKER

The main point in this fourth chapter is this: How do you help people who are experiencing brokenness and pain?

Based upon his experience, Pastor Mike offered ten things that we often do when people are dealing with tough situations. To see the big picture, fill out the following chart.

In the "Suggested Action" column, identify the specific action that Pastor Mike listed. In the next column, jot down an example or two of what *you* would do personally for someone you loved who is experiencing brokenness and pain.

#	SUGGESTED ACTION	EXAMPLES OF IT
1		
2		

#	SUGGESTED ACTION	EXAMPLES OF IT
3		
4		
5		
6		
7		
8		
9		
10		

From the chart, identify the suggested action with which you are most comfortable. Explain why you feel that way.

From the chart, identify the suggested action that you would find most difficult. Explain why you feel that way.

Pastor Mike also mentioned that the some of the suggestions on this list could backfire. Choose one or more that you think could backfire and explain what the risk is.

When Job's three friends, Eliphaz, Bildad, and Zophar, heard about all the tragedy and pain that Job was suffering, they all agreed to do three things.

What were the three things they agreed to do?

1.

2.

3.

When the three friends arrived, they didn't recognize Job. They sat down on the ground with him and didn't say a word for seven days. What are your thoughts about the three friends just sitting there for a week without saying anything?

The book of Job is so relatable to our lives. We may be in Job's shoes. On the other hand, we may be in the shoes of the friends.

Is there anyone in your life who needs you to come along their side, to sympathize with them, and to comfort them?

Pastor Mike mentioned that "after tragedy, community is a necessity." What did he mean by that?

Pastor Mike also mentioned that "after tragedy, community is messy." What did he mean by that?

Pastor Mike gave some applications for those who are in the shoes of the friends seeking to help a friend who is experiencing brokenness and pain. Jot down for yourself what you find helpful to remember.

Pastor Mike gave some applications for those in Job's shoes who have friends seeking to ease their brokenness and pain. Jot down for yourself what you find helpful to remember.

What is the most significant takeaway from chapter 4 for you?

- CHAPTER 5 -

GOD WON'T TELL ME WHY THERE'S PAIN?

I've learned over the years of being a pastor that when we're in pain, the most natural question for us to ask is actually the most dangerous question for us to ask. The question that instinctively, logically, naturally comes out of our hearts is actually the question that can mess with our faith in a profound way. And I thought about that when many of my church members told me their stories of pain and suffering.

A couple weeks ago, I sent a survey to our church family. The survey had two questions. What is the hardest thing you've ever been through in life? How did you react to it spiritually?

When those surveys came in, I read about what our church members have been through. Tough childhoods, traumatic experiences, abuse, parents splitting up at a young age, a loved one dying too young, dyslexia, anxiety that doesn't let go, depression that comes back in vicious cycles. I learned about the struggles in high school and young adult life. There were all these heartbreaking stories, but when people got to the second question—How did you react spiritually?—one particular question came up. And it didn't just come up on one or two surveys. Many said it was their gut reaction to the suffering. It was a question of just one word: *Why?* Why did someone get cancer? Why was there a car accident? Why did this happen to me? Why didn't my marriage make it? Why can't I find someone? Why can't we have a baby? Why is this happening? Why am I going through this? Why is God doing this or sending this or permitting this or allowing this? Why did I have to go through something so difficult? Why?

WHY DID I HAVE TO GO THROUGH SOMETHING SO DIFFICULT?

It's a natural question. It's the question we all ask, but I want to pose to you that it's actually a spiritually dangerous question because of the two ways most people answer it. This is important—I think maybe the number-one way people answer the why question is this: Maybe you're going through such pain because you are bad. You're suffering, and maybe the reason is because God is trying to get you back for what you did.

Back when I was a kid, I watched *Saturday Night Live.* There was a skit in the early '90s called "Deep Thoughts With Jack Handy." Do you remember that? Picture meditation music and scrolling lyrics. Jack Handy had these deep thoughts about life. One I remember is this: "If a kid asks where rain comes from, I think a cute thing to tell him is, 'God is crying.' And if he asks why God is crying, another cute thing to tell him is, 'It's probably because of something you did.'" It was not just mean and kind of funny; there's some truth to that, right? If it feels like God is disappointed, he's crying. If the rain is coming down on life, if it's difficult, the instinctive thing we think is that we must have done something wrong. "What did I do? Why is God getting back at me?" I remember thinking this when I had the flu as a kid. You know, sitting in the bathroom, throwing up: "God, I don't know what I did, but I promise I'll be . . ." We just think that our suffering is so intimately connected with our sin.

Here's why we think that: Because it mostly is, right? You don't have to be a Bible person to believe that when you make bad choices, you often end up with a bad life. If you're partying through every weekend, don't be shocked when you wake up with a hangover. The physical pain and suffering aren't parts of some mysterious plan of God; that's just you being dumb. If you are bossy and controlling in your relationship and it ends up a mess, maybe you had it coming. If you totally ignore God and his amazing promises to watch over you and protect you and instead soak in news that the sky is falling, the world is pointless, and everyone hates each other, you will feel anxious at the end of the day. Maybe that's because you made bad choices. In the Bible, the book of Proverbs talks about this all the time. There is often a connection between personal sin and personal suffering. So it's not crazy when life is hard that we might think there must be some connection to what we did.

But here's a problem: There's often a connection between sin and suffering, but there's not always a connection between sin and suffering. An innocent little kid is hurt by a family member. A ten-year-old gets cancer. A random car wreck changes a family forever. That's not the same as getting drunk and then having a hangover. It's not the same as being argumentative and no one wants to be around you. When bad stuff is random, people struggle with the only other logical answer . . .

God is bad. It's incredibly logical, right? If God is supposedly present everywhere, knows everything, and can do anything, then why can't he fix your personal suffering? If you're a little kid who can't sleep because anxiety is churning in your stomach and supposedly God is present, supposedly he knows exactly how hard it is for you, and supposedly he has the power to fix it and he doesn't, it's not crazy to think that's bad. You wouldn't do that. If you knew a heartbroken family whose kid was just in an accident and you could push a button and fix it, would you just look at the button and not push it? Everyone in the room would say, "That's bad. You're bad." This is a logical struggle that leads many, many people to question the goodness of God and even the existence of God. Meet an intelligent atheist, ask her why she doesn't believe there is a God, and I can almost guarantee this will be in her top three: How can a good God exist in a world that is so broken and painful? If God is loving and could change it but he doesn't, how can you believe that God is still good?

Do you see why the most natural question is the most dangerous question? You suffer. I suffer. We go through pain. Are we bad? Is God mad? Should we feel guilty or shameful? Should we disconnect from faith? shake a fist at heaven? deny his existence? move on with this life? It's a real struggle, it's an intense struggle, and it's a struggle that has existed for a long, long time.

HOW CAN A GOOD GOD EXIST?

We've been studying the book of Job. It's a book of wisdom that's tucked inside about the middle of our Bibles. The book of Job is essentially about the love of God. Will we love God when life is hard? Can we be sure that God loves us when life is hard? But if you've read the book of Job before, you know the bulk of it is really about this question: Why? There's this guy Job, his life is falling apart, he's lost his health, he's lost his wealth, and all ten of his children die in a tragic accident. His three friends show up, and a fourth friend shows up later. When these five guys get together in the same room and start talking to each other, the question they want to answer is this: Why did this happen? "Job, why did you lose everything? Why are your children gone?" They lift their eyes to the heavens and ask the same thing you and I would: *Why?*

It's quite a discussion because it doesn't take just a verse or a chapter in the book of Job; it spans from Job chapter 3 all the way through Job chapter 37. Thirty-five straight chapters of the Bible that try to answer the why question. I'm not going to write about every chapter, but I do want to show what happens when we answer the why question in the wrong way. And then I want to show you some little nuggets of wisdom that are packed inside of this book that you might have missed. They might help you the next time you ask the question, "Why?"

If you want a good summary for Job chapters 3–37, Google "Job by William Blake." He was an artist in the 1800s. If you look at that picture, it's not hard to guess how Job's friends answered the why question. Look at those pointing fingers! They had come to comfort him, but when the question needed to be answered of why this happened to Job, this was their accusation: "Because you must be bad, Job."

Let me machine-gun a bunch of verses from this 35-chapter argument to you. One of Job's friends, a man named Eliphaz, says this: **"As I have observed, those who plow evil and those who sow trouble reap it"** (4:8). It's a bit poetic. You hear what he's saying? "Reap what you sow. Why do you have all this trouble? Because you started it." Ouch. It gets worse when his friend Bildad opens his mouth. He says, **"When your children sinned against [God], he gave them over to the penalty of their sin"** (8:4). "Why are your children dead? Because they were bad." Zophar, his other friend, adds this: **"Know this: God has even forgotten some of your sin"** (11:6). "I know your body's covered in boils, I know all ten of your children are dead, I know you've lost everything you had, but I think God forgot half of the bad stuff that you did. You should have it worse."

Job is in intense pain; he knows that none of this is true. He fires back in Job chapter 9: **"How can mere mortals prove their innocence before God?"** (verse 2). "How can I prove to you none of this is true? I'm innocent; I didn't do anything wrong. And he says in Job 6:24: **"Teach me, and I will be quiet; show me where I have been wrong."** "You accuse me and my children of sinning. Can you bring the proof? Do you remember the time? Can you present your evidence?"

And because Job knows he hasn't done anything wrong, nothing that would match up with this kind of suffering, what he ends up doing is turning on God. And he says, "Man, I wish I could bring God to court. If he wasn't a coward who hides himself up in heaven, I would go on the prosecution and accuse him. I don't deserve this. I didn't sin. Why am I suffering?" And when Job says that, that maybe God is bad, his friends lose it. One of his friends says this: **"Why has your heart carried you away, and why do your eyes flash, so that you vent your rage against God and pour out such words from your mouth?"** (15:12,13). Job's exhausted by it, so he replies, **"Will your longwinded speeches never end?"** (16:3).

So Bildad fires back, **"Why are we regarded as cattle and considered stupid in your sight?"** (18:3). And Job fires back, **"Have you never questioned those who travel? Have you paid no regard to their accounts— that the wicked are spared from the day of calamity?"** (21:29,30). "Wait, if bad people have it good, then maybe the system doesn't work like you think. If villains get away with it, if the guys who are jerks get the girl, then maybe the world doesn't function like you assume." And so his friends fire back. Eliphaz says, **"Is not your wickedness great? Are not your sins endless? You demanded security from your relatives for no reason; you stripped people of their clothing, leaving them naked"** (22:5,6). Job knows that's a lie. So he doubles down and says, **"I will never admit you are in the right; till I die, I will not deny my integrity"** (27:5).

It's like the comment section on Facebook, right? You're dumb. No, you're dumb. No, you are. No, you are. They're like grown men who are children, four guys just going at it. You're bad; no, God is bad. Don't say God is bad; that's bad. Well, you're bad because you talk too much. Well, you're bad because you said God isn't talking enough. They go back and forth and back and forth and back and forth until the fifth guy shows up. Apparently, he's a younger guy. He's been listening to these old dudes duke it out for too long, and now he knows, he's shown them respect, and it's his turn to speak.

His name is Elihu. And you know it's going to be

rough because at one point he says this: **"Be assured that my words are not false; one who has perfect knowledge is with you"** (36:4). I dare you to say that to your dad: "Dad, you might want to get out your pen. I'm about to talk, and it's going to be awesome." So what's Elihu's perfect knowledge? He's pretty smart for a young guy, so he thinks. How's he going to answer the why question? Well, here's what he says: **"[God] repays everyone for what they have done; he brings on them what their conduct deserves. It is unthinkable that God would do wrong, that the Almighty would pervert justice"** (34:11,12). In Elihu's mind, there are only two answers: "God unjust? Unthinkable. So you are getting what your conduct deserves. You looked good, but you were hiding something. Everyone thought you were such a good guy, but God could see your heart. He knows you're bad, and that's why you're going through such a bad time of life."

You can read the rest if you want to, all 35 chapters of it. I've given you the lowlights of the conversation. But if you do read it, you might wonder why this is in the Bible. The Bible only has so many chapters and verses and pages. Why would God waste 35 chapters on five men arguing? The answer is this: Because when you and I insist on trying to figure out why, it all goes wrong. We hear something bad has happened to someone, maybe a friend is getting a divorce, and we start to think, "I wonder what they did?" Or we go through some physical suffering, like me as a little kid with the flu, and we wonder, "God, I don't know what it is, but it must be something. Forgive me." Or like an atheist, we shake our heads and our fists at the heavens and wonder if God is the same God we believed in when we were little kids. The book of Job is a massive warning about what happens when we insist on knowing why.

You might be tempted to skim through it, but it's worth your time because nestled in the middle of these long-winded arguments are two truths that can actually help you when you don't understand why. In Job chapter 28, there's what my Bible calls an interlude about wisdom. The chapter is kind of a weird chapter; it talks about copper and iron and silver and gold and how you don't find the chunks of gold just here on the ground; it's actually buried way, way, way deep in the dirt. You can't see it; it's almost impossible to find it. All the birds can see so much of the world, but they can't see it. And then there's this section: **"Where then does wisdom come from? Where does understanding dwell? It is hidden from the eyes of every living thing, concealed even from the birds in the sky. . . . God understands the way to it and he alone knows where it dwells"** (28:20,21,23). So where is the answer? How are you going to understand why you went through that physically or financially or relationally? In your marriage, with your body, with whatever, with our world, the answer is hidden. It's like a diamond buried somewhere in the ground that you will never see. God sees it. He knows the answer. But God has not chosen to reveal it. Therefore, you and I don't know it.

It's hard to swallow, but I want you to write this down. This book of wisdom from the Old Testament answers the question, Why do I have this pain? Here's the biblical answer: We don't know why. We could guess, but that would be dangerous. We could assume, but that might be dumb. Read the Bible, cover to cover, and you will not find out why. Study Greek and Hebrew, like the pastors from our church who can get to the original language of the Scriptures; you still won't know why. Start from the front cover, and make it all the way to the back past the maps. Do you know where you will find the answer to your specific pain? You won't.

So I want you to practice with me the wisest answer to the why question. I'm going to pose a bunch of questions, and I want you to give me the biblically wisest answer, all right?

Why do some people lose their parents when they are just little kids?
I don't know.

Why do some people struggle with anxiety from their earlier memories?
I don't know.

Why are there some really, really amazing women who can't conceive children?

I don't know.

Why are there car accidents with people who were
the best people in town?
I don't know.

Why did you go through that one year of your life
that you wish you could redo?
I don't know.

Why was there that one season of pain that you
just did not get?
I don't know.

I don't know. I wish I did. If I knew, I'd tell you. If we
could dig down and find it like a chunk of gold, we'd dig
for it. But God alone knows the answer to that question.
You and I can guess all day long, and maybe some of the
guesses will make us feel better. Maybe God allowed you
to battle depression because he wanted to take that mess
and turn it into a ministry. He wanted to use you to reach
out to someone who was depressed and it wouldn't have
worked if you wouldn't have understood what it's like to
be there. Maybe God had a purpose for that. Maybe he
knew that that doctor or nurse didn't even believe in God
and he wanted to use your faithfulness and your suffering in the hospital room so they would look at it and say,
"I don't have that." Maybe that was his purpose. Maybe
God let that person in your family die because he knew

that your cousin would come to the funeral and finally realize that what matters in the end is not your money, not your body, not your job. It's your faith in Jesus, and it was that spark that got your cousin back closer to God. Maybe that was the reason, but I don't know for sure.

My little brother died at six weeks old. Why did God do that to my parents? We have a guess. My mom thinks that after Jimmy died, she held me so tightly and raised me up to know Jesus. It's possible that I'm a pastor today because that happened to my brother but, honestly, I don't know. And neither do you.

So if we don't know why, why would we trust God? It's pretty convenient, right? If you were dating someone and they weren't there for you when you needed them, you might say, "Well, why didn't you help?" If they said, "I'm not going to tell you," you'd be out of that relationship, right? Why would you trust a person who doesn't tell you what they know? We find that same answer in the book of Job. In the midst of the ups and downs of his faith, his yelling at God, questioning God, accusing God, Job actually gives us this answer. He says, "We don't know why, but we do know who." Job says we don't know why this happened, but we do know who God is. God has not revealed why he didn't stop this pain, but he has revealed many things about himself. And if we know who God is, if we know what God is like, then we learn to take a deep breath and trust that he's God. A God

WE DO KNOW WHO GOD IS.

we can trust. A God we don't have to question. The Bible would say, "Be still and know that he's God."

When my daughters were little, Kim and I took them to the doctor for their checkups and their shots. We stood there as this strange woman whom we'd just met uncapped a needle and plunged it into the fat thigh of one of our little girls. Have you ever seen a kid whose mouth screams about three seconds before the voice comes out? The eyes get huge with tears, and though our daughter couldn't say it at the time, she looked at us with an expression that said, "Why? Why aren't you stopping this, Dad? Who is this woman? Why is she stabbing me, and why are you smiling?" In fact, we weren't just watching, we were holding down those little legs so they could be stabbed again. We didn't tell her why. A little kid doesn't get how medicine or the human body works. In those moments, all we could depend on was that she didn't know why but she did know who. The dad who was holding her down was the dad who just snuggled with her in her jammies that morning. The mom who was standing by, not stopping it, was the same mom who gave life to her, who fed her, who cleaned up her messes, who kissed her on the forehead, who read little books to her in her lap. She didn't get why, but we hope that she got who.

And I hope you do too. You could go to church for the rest of your life. You could watch *Time of Grace* on TV until the day you die, but you will not find out the reason why a certain thing happened to you. But if you keep going to church, if you keep reading the Bible, if you keep watching, you will find out something: *Who.*

Here's how Job put it in the midst of his mess. He said, **"I know that my redeemer lives, and that in the end he will stand on the earth. And after my skin has been destroyed, yet in my flesh I will see God; I myself will see him with my own eyes—I, and not another. How my heart yearns within me!"** (Job 19:25–27). I love that! "Here's what I know," Job said. "I don't know why God is doing this. I don't get it. I'm frustrated with God, but I do know this: I know that my Redeemer lives."

Christians in pain have been saying that for the past two thousand years. What you're going through right now, what you have been through, there have been countless Christians who have gotten through that valley because they said, "I know who." They said, "I don't know why, but I do know who. I don't know why this is happening, but I know that my God is worthy of praise. I don't know why he's not stopping this, but I do know the kind of God whom I worship. He is my Redeemer."

The word *Redeemer* is a fancy Bible word. It literally means "to pay a price to get something back." If a company gives you a coupon, you can redeem it; they will pay you a price, the discount, to get the coupon back. Job said, "Here's what I know: I know that I have a Redeemer. I have a God who paid a price to get something back." That sound familiar? "I don't know why, but I do know who. I know Jesus, the Savior, who redeemed me. I do know

Jesus, the one who suffered something even worse for me. I do know that there is a God who didn't just give me a second chance; he paid the whole debt so I could be called his child. I do know a Jesus who died on a cross for my sins, and now he lives, risen on the third day. I do know that Jesus clothed me so perfectly in his holy garments that I will see God. I won't be kicked outside the gates; I won't be condemned to hell. I will see him with my own eyes. I will stand before him and rejoice. I don't know why I suffered, but I do know who suffered for me." That's what Job knew. Do you?

How could God be bad if he sent his Son for us? I don't know your story, but in my life I haven't been to prison, I haven't been arrested, but I have done a thousand things I would be ashamed for you to know. But God loves me. There are sins you'd rather forget; there are secrets you might be keeping. God knows all of it and yet, he loves you. We were not God's BFFs but his enemies, just **HE SENT HIS SON FOR US.** living for ourselves, ignoring the Bible, ignoring prayer, and God's response to that kind of rebellion was to send a Redeemer. He cannot be bad. Someone who loves their enemies cannot be bad. Someone who gives us a thousand chances to hear the good news and believe it cannot be bad, so here's the deal. I don't know why, but I do know who. I hope you don't suffer today or this week or this year. But if you do, don't waste your time. We don't know why. Instead, fix your eyes on who—the Savior who loved you so much that he went through something worse than Job. The Savior who has risen from the grave so that you could have the hope of eternal life without pain. He is the Savior who is with you, walking through the valley of the shadow of death so you will fear no evil.

PRAYER

Dear God, I wish you'd just tell me why. It seems like a reasonable thing to do, but you don't. It would be insane for me to think that I know better. It would be arrogant for me to assume that I could be God and do it better than you do. So give me the kind of humility it takes to accept your nonanswer.

The devil would love me to answer the why question in these ways: to think that I'm not forgiven, that you're mad at me, that you're still punishing me, or there's something I did that Jesus didn't. Or he would love me to turn on you, to question you, to doubt you, to be frustrated with you instead of being grateful for you. God, lead me away from those two temptations. Deliver me from that evil as I let the question go and trust that you love me.

Jesus, if you came and taught me a bunch of rules, I probably couldn't trust God. But since you came to seek and save people who were lost, since you lived a holy life so I could be clothed in you, since you died to take away every stain and sin, and since you rose from the grave to prove that is true, I can trust you today. Truly you are my loving Savior and my loving Lord.

So I'm asking you, Holy Spirit, to give me faith. Jesus, you said in this world we would have many troubles, and I am living proof. But you will never leave me; you will never forsake me, and one day you and I will stand upon the earth glorious and new. I will not regret saying, "I don't know why, but I do know who." I pray all these things, Jesus, in your beautiful name. Amen.

FOR FURTHER STUDY:
GOD WON'T TELL ME WHY THERE'S PAIN?
DR. BRUCE BECKER

Pastor Mike began this chapter with these words: "I've learned over the years of being a pastor that when you're in pain, the most natural question for you to ask is actually the most dangerous question for you to ask."

What was this natural but dangerous question?

⸻

Pastor Mike indicated that this is a natural question to ask but, because of the two perspectives people have in answering the question, it becomes a spiritually dangerous question to ask.

First perspective

Summarize for yourself or share with others in your group what the *first perspective* is when people ask, "Why?"

Why is this first perspective *mostly right*?

But what makes this first perspective so spiritually dangerous?

Have you ever asked the why question in this way? If so, give an example from your life experience.

Second perspective

Summarize for yourself or share with others in your group what the second perspective is when people ask, "Why?"

What makes this second perspective *incredibly logical?*

But what makes this second perspective so spiritually dangerous?

Have you ever asked the why question in this way? If so, give an example from your life experience.

Beginning with Job chapter 3, this is the question Job and his friends repeatedly ask—Why? For 35 straight chapters, Job and his friends ask this question from either the first or the second perspective.

Let's take a quick trip through these 35 chapters. Along the way, let's consider a few statements made by Job and his friends. Evaluate whether the statement is more aligned with the first perspective or with the second perspective.

Eliphaz: **"As I have observed, those who plow**

evil and those who sow trouble reap it. At the breath of God they perish" (4:8,9).

Job: "If I have sinned, what have I done to you, you who see everything we do? Why have you made me your target?" (7:20).

Bildad: "When your children sinned against him, he gave them over to the penalty of their sin" (8:4).

Job: "How can mere mortals prove their innocence before God? Though they wished to dispute with him, they could not answer him one time out of a thousand" (9:2,3).

Zophar: "Know this: God has even forgotten some of your sin" (11:6).

Job: "Show me my offense and my sin. Why do you hide your face and consider me your enemy?" (13:23,24).

Eliphaz: "Your sin prompts your mouth; you adopt the tongue of the crafty" (15:5).

Job: "God has turned me over to the ungodly and thrown me into the clutches of the wicked" (16:11).

This back-and-forth dialogue continues for another 15

chapters until Job stops speaking with his friends.

What is the contrast between how Job's friends were answering the why question and how Job was answering the question?

In Job chapter 32, we meet another person. His name is Elihu. He is a younger man with the opinion that he is the only one with perfect knowledge. His message is summed up in these words: **"Far be it from God to do evil, from the Almighty to do wrong. He repays everyone for what they have done; he brings upon them what their conduct deserves"** (Job 34:10,11).

Job claimed his innocence and believed God was wronging him. How did Elihu respond to Job's claims?

Pastor Mike revealed why there are 35 chapters of back-and-forth dialogue trying to answer the why question. Consider for yourself or discuss with others in your group what Pastor Mike said: "The book of Job is a massive warning about what happens when we insist on knowing why."

Pastor Mike then went on to say: "This book of wisdom from the Old Testament answers the question, Why do I have this pain? Here's the biblical answer: We don't know why."

What does the answer "we don't know why" mean for us when we experience brokenness and pain in our lives?

———

What does this answer mean when we come alongside others who are experiencing brokenness and pain?

———

In the middle of the dialogue between Job and his friends, Job changed his focus from the "why" to the "who": **"I know that my redeemer lives, and that in the end he will stand on the earth. And after my skin has been destroyed, yet in my flesh I will see God; I myself will see him with my own eyes—I, and not another. How my heart yearns within me!"** (Job 19:25-27).

When we or others experience brokenness and pain in our lives, what comfort do these words of Job provide us?

———

What is the most significant takeaway from this fifth chapter for you?

- CHAPTER 6 -

GOD'S NONANSWER
IS THE ANSWER?

I recently had a conversation with a guy I had never met before. Someone who watches our church services online had given him my number. I talked to this guy on the phone one afternoon, and before I hung up the phone, I found out that he and I had an uncanny amount of things in common. In the course of the conversation, I found out that his hometown was the exact same place where I grew up. He graduated the exact year I graduated high school. He played soccer too. And it turns out this guy and I were literally on the same soccer field playing against each other 20-25 years ago. We had this insane amount of things in common except for one big thing.

As soon as I hung up the phone that afternoon, I went home where my wife was waiting with dinner and our weekly Friday date night. When he hung up the phone, he continued sitting in a very quiet house because his young wife had just died. She died out of the blue; no one saw it coming. Something went wrong; one moment they were making plans for the future, and then she was gone.

I obviously can't share a lot about the conversation he and I had, but I think it's safe to say that the question he asked me, the reason he wanted to talk to a pastor he didn't even know, was because he was wondering the exact same thing that I would have been wondering if I were him. He was wondering, "Why? Pastor, why did this happen? Out of all the people in

WHEN LIFE IS HARD, WE NEED A WHY. the world, my wife was an amazing person. Why her? Out of all the couples in the world, we were happy together; not every couple is. Why us?" His heart was aching for an explanation to the tragedy that had happened; he was wondering why.

It's the most natural question in the world when you're in pain, isn't it? In fact, take note of this next thing because I think it's so true of your heart, of my heart, and of this poor man's heart. When life is hard, we need a *why*. I might not know you personally, but I bet I could predict this: that you have been able to get through some really difficult seasons of life because you had a good reason why. When people have a reason why, they don't turn on God, shake their fists at the heavens, or question their faith altogether because life is hard. Think about school. How many painful mornings did you wake up? How many thousands of hours did you study things you had no interest in? How many tests, how many exams, how many years did you sit in an uncomfortable desk? But you did it even though it was painful because there was a good reason why; you knew that the education and the graduation might lead to a scholarship or to college or to a good job, a good salary, a better life. You went through that pain because you understood why.

Or think about sports. Did you have a coach who would made you run? We called them suicides back in the day; you sprinted and sprinted and sprinted more and sprinted so much more. You gasped and felt like dying. But you did it, and you came back the next day for practice. Why did you do it? Because there was a reason why. You wanted to be faster and stronger; you wanted to outlast the team in the big game. You wanted to make it to the playoffs. You and I can go through physical suffering if there's a reason why.

Or think about childbirth. I don't want to make any women reading this relive the trauma, but do you remember it? Do you remember the morning sickness and the feet that swell up and the clothes that don't fit and trying to sleep while the kid who looks so cute in the 4D ultrasound is like an MMA fighter, punching the inside of your uterus? The physics of this baffles me. You physically pushed the child out of your body and yet, you didn't lose your faith . . . because there was a good reason why.

We can get through hard seasons of life—like labor pain, agonizing suffering—as long as there's a good enough reason, as long as we understand why. We get the pain of education. We get the pain of athletics. We get the pain of childbirth, but sometimes we go through things in life that don't have such an obvious explanation. You haven't called me on the phone like that guy from that Friday afternoon, but you've wondered the same things: "Why would this happen? And out of all the people in the world, why did it have to happen to me?" Maybe this goes back to childhood. Why wasn't your dad there? Why did he create you and then not want to raise you? You didn't do anything wrong. Some kids have amazing families, parents who are together, but why not you? Or you had a father who was there and maybe you wish he wasn't. He was physically aggressive, emotionally distant, or supposed to be a little glimpse of our Father in heaven but was just the opposite. You see some kids playing catch with their dad in the backyard, but that wasn't your childhood. Why?

Some kids do fine in school. It's like they show up without studying for the test and then ace it, but you're the kid who struggled to read, to understand, to remember; you're always behind even though you put in the effort. Why is that? Some people never have to deal with anxiety their whole lives. They fall asleep easily, but not you. And you wonder why? "God, I pray about this all the time; why doesn't this just go away?" I could add to the questions, right? Why is depression part of some of our stories? Why are there car accidents and cancer? Why do some of our parents and grandparents and best friends die young? Why do some of us want love but can't find it? Why do some of us think we've found love and then it slips through our fingers? Or we take our vows for better or worse and then the vows are broken? We want to have children, but we can't? "God, just tell me a reason why, and I can get through it."

But that's the problem, right? The honest truth is that we don't know why. When that guy called me up, I tried to listen. I tried to offer some Scripture to him, but at the end of the day, his basic visceral question was, "Why did this happen to me?" I couldn't answer. And that's the struggle with some of our pain. We need a why, but we can't find it. There's only one person who really knows why life is the way it is, and we don't exactly get one-on-one conversations with him.

But that's what makes the book of Job so absurdly fascinating. At the very end of Job, this Old Testament book about pain and suffering, God, the only one who knows why, shows up to talk to Job, the one who needed an answer why. The book of Job is 42 chapters long. For about 35 of those chapters, Job and his friends argue about why this is happening. Is Job bad? Is God bad? They can't figure it out; it's a total mess. So in chapter 38 through chapter 42, God comes down and has a face-to-face conversation with his dear friend Job.

What happens in that conversation is not at all what you would expect, but if you or someone you love is suffering deeply, it's exactly what you need. We're going to fly through the last five chapters of the book of Job as we search for the question we all want answered: Why?

Let's kick things off with Job 38:1-3: **"Then the LORD spoke to Job out of the storm. He said: 'Who is this that obscures my plans with words without knowledge? Brace yourself like a man; I will question you, and you shall answer me.'"** Oh. God shows up in a storm. Have you ever gotten caught in a fierce storm? Boom—skies turn black; whoosh, rain comes down; lightning flashes; and the thunder cracks—and that's kind of the point.

God shows up, not as a little baby but in the midst of a fierce storm. He wants to remind Job before he says a word about the point he is just about to make. Just in case Job doesn't pick up on the meaning, God says this: "Brace yourself like a man. Did you bring your helmet today, Job? You're going to need it. You've been asking me a lot of questions; you and your friends have had a lot of words. Now it's my turn. I am going to question you, and you will answer me." I won't quote every verse that comes next, but for the next two chapters, God intellectually eviscerates Job. I went through my Bible and circled every question mark. In Job 38 through 42, I found 77 separate questions that God asks Job. He booms question after question, giving Job this pop quiz on how much he actually knows about the way the world works. And Job? Job doesn't do so well. He scores a 0 out of 77. If he was in fourth grade, he would have missed his next recess to study again for the test.

Let me give you just a little glimpse of the kind of questions that God asks Job. He says, **"Where were you** when I laid the earth's foundation? Tell me, if you un-derstand" (Job 38:4). A few verses later he says, **"Have you comprehended the vast expanses of the earth? Tell me, if you know all this"** (verse 18). A few verses later he says, **"Surely you know, for you were already born! You have lived so many years!"** (verse 21). That's God being sarcastic, by the way. And God keeps going. He says, "Job, do you know how storms work? Can you predict their path better than the best meteorologist?" And Job stares up at the storm. "How about ostriches," God says to Job. "Do you know why they work the way they do? Why they're shaped the way that they are? Why they run fast? Because I do." Question, after question, after question. First 10, then 30, then 50, then 70, then 77 times in a row, Job shrugs his shoulders. He doesn't know.

Note that God has not told Job why he lost his health or his wealth or his sons or his daughters. God has just shown Job time and time again that Job maybe doesn't know quite as much as he thought. And so, here's Job's response: **"Then Job answered the LORD: 'I am unworthy—how can I reply to you? I put my hand over my mouth. I spoke once, but I have no** **HE IS NOT WORTHY TO JUDGE GOD.** **answer—twice, but I will say no more'"** (Job 40:3-5). As Job stares up at the storm, as he thinks a little more crit-ically about what he knows and how much God knows, he realizes that he is not worthy to judge God. He's not worthy to demand a reason from God. He actually claps his hand over his mouth and says, "I spoke once, but I'm not going to do it again."

But apparently God isn't done. At this point, I would say, "Well good, Job, I'm glad you get it." But that's not what God does. **"Then the LORD spoke to Job out of the storm: 'Brace yourself like a man; I will question you, and you shall answer me. Would you discredit my justice? Would you condemn me to justify yourself?'"** (Job 40:6–8). "Is that what you're going to do, Job? You're going to say that you're bad? You don't know the difference between right and wrong? You would condemn me as being an unworthy, unloving, unkind Creator just to prove to your friends that you're not a bad guy. Is that what you're doing?"

The first time I read this, I thought God was being kind of mean. I mean, Job said he was sorry; he said he wouldn't question God again. And God comes back for round two. It might seem mean, but I can tell you this: It was not. From the very first page of the book, we know that God loves Job. He's so proud of his son Job that he's boasting in front of the devil. So what is God doing? One blogger said that what God is doing with Job is kind of what Gandalf the Great did with Bilbo Baggins in *The Hobbit*. There's this scene where Gandalf, who's a powerful wizard, is talking to his hobbit friend, Bilbo Baggins. Bilbo is in the possession of a very powerful magic ring, and Gandalf is trying to convince him to get rid of it. He's seen the evil magic that is contained within the ring; he's worried about what it will do to Bilbo's heart. But Bilbo, who's under the influence of the dark magic, actually turns on his old friend Gandalf. He grows suspicious of his intentions. He maybe thinks that Gandalf wants him to get rid of it so he can pick it up and steal it. And he gets aggressive and questioning and doubtful. In fact, he reaches for his little hobbit sword to fight against his old friend. So do you know what Gandalf does? He goes off. Gandalf the Great proves his greatness. He steps closer and towers over the little hobbit. He gets big and his eyes flash with rage and he says, "Bilbo Baggins, if you say that again, I shall get angry." And seeing the rage in his eyes, Bilbo snaps out of the spell. Gandalf takes a step back and says, "I'm trying to help you. I wish you would trust me like you used to."

That's what God is doing with Job. Job, in his pain and suffering, is questioning the God who loves him, who made him, who blesses him. He doesn't understand the reasons why, so now he's questioning the very heart of God. He's discrediting God's kindness and love. He's actually condemning God for not being as loving as he claimed to be, so God gets big. He says, "Job, uh-uh. I'm trying to help you. Sin is corrupting your heart, and I have to remind you that I am God and you are not."

That's why in the next two chapters, God starts round two. This time he doesn't pepper Job with as many questions as he previously did. He instead gives two examples of these immense beasts that would have terrified Job. In

Job chapters 40 and 41, they are called the behemoth and the leviathan. Now if you read the descriptions in these chapters, it seems like one is a massive mega-crocodile and the other is a fierce, aggressive hippopotamus. Some people think they seem bigger than that; they might be extinct species. Some people actually think these are mythical descriptions of huge beasts that Job could never fight against. But God's point is this: "Job, if you came face-to-face with these two beasts, you would feel very, very small. But when these two beasts come face-to-face with me, they feel very, very small. You've been questioning me like I'm your equal, like you have the right to judge me; let me give you an example to prove that you are not."

It would be a good idea for you to take a few moments to read chapters 40 and 41. Here's my favorite line from God: **"Can you make a pet of** [this beast] **like a bird or put it on a leash for the young women in your house?"** (Job 41:5). God's asking, "Would you like a crocodile for a pet? Would you let it sleep on the end of your bed? No, you'd be terrified, but it doesn't bother me. Would you stick a fierce, aggressive hippo in a little swimming pool with your sons? your daughters? Would you put it on a leash or walk it around the block? Because I can. I'm God. I'm not you, Job. I'm bigger, I'm stronger, I'm better, I'm holier, I know more, I can do more, and I love more. You are not like me. I am God, and you are not."

And it works. Finally in the last chapter of the book, here's how Job replies: **"Then Job replied to the Lord: 'I** know that you can do all things; no purpose of yours can be thwarted. You asked, "Who is this that obscures my plans without knowledge?" Surely I spoke of things I did not understand, things too wonderful for me to know. You said, "Listen now, and I will speak; I will question you, and you shall answer me." My ears had heard of you but now my eyes have seen you. Therefore I despise myself and repent in dust and ashes'" (42:1-6).

Job repents. That's the Bible's way of saying he changed directions. He was thinking this and then: "No, no, no; now I think that." You can read the conclusion of the story in a little epilogue at the end of chapter 42. God shows up and sets things straight. He restores Job's health, and he gives him back his wealth; in fact, twice as much. He blesses him with a new family: sons and daughters. In the last verse of the book of Job, Job dies an old man. Best of all, he is filled with faith and love for God.

But here's the fascinating part: Job never gets an answer. God doesn't show up and say, "Okay, I'm God; you're not, and now, Job, here's my playbook. Here's this conversation you didn't hear between me and Satan. Here's exactly why I let that happen. Here's how I'm going to use your story for generations to come to help people who are suffering." God never once says a word about any of it. He just shows up and says, "God!" And that was good for Job. He said, "My ears had heard of you, God. I thought I knew you, but now my eyes have seen you. So I repent because seeing you, just remembering who, that's enough."

That is a profound lesson for you and me. We think we need a reason why. We think that if God would just say this or that, just explain why this path and not that one, but it's not true. According to the story of a man who suffered much more intensely than we will likely suffer, we don't need a why; we just need to remember who. You might think I'm being repetitive, but write this down or highlight it right in the book. It's actually a two-part answer. The key is to remember who and Who. Yes, I mean *who* with a small *w* and *Who* with a capital *W*. The ending of the book of Job is about remembering who you are and who God is. If you remember those two things, then you won't need an answer to that big question: *Why?*

So let's start with who. Do you know who you are? Do you know who I am? I am a 41-year-old man who doesn't remember what he had for breakfast three days ago. I'm a middle-aged guy who despite all his education can't verify my usernames and passwords. I spend about two hours a week just guessing which of the passwords goes with a certain account. What do you and I know about ourselves or the world or the way the universe works? We might feel big when we compare ourselves to our classmates, coworkers, and family members, but what do we know about life?

Let me prove it to you. I want you to think of someone you know. Anyone. Now I want you to guess how many hairs are on that person's head. The answer, if my research is correct, if you are thinking of a brunette, is about 100,000. If you're thinking of a blonde, the answer on average is 150,000. What about their eyebrows? How many individual hairs are in their eyebrows. The answer is, on average, 600.

Here's my point: Do you even know how many hairs are on your own head? Do you know how many breaths you've taken since breakfast? Do you know how many times your own heart has beaten today to keep you alive? If you didn't have a Fitbit or an iPhone, would you know how many steps you've taken since last Friday? The point is that when it comes to you and me, we have no clue. Before I get big and start questioning God, it's pretty humbling to know it's my hair and I don't even know. It's my heart, my lungs, my whatever; I don't even know these little things about my own life. I am so unqualified to understand the big picture of what God does with pain and suffering as he runs the universe. It's like when a one-year old keeps asking, "No? Why?" As a parent, you say, "I know more than you!" Or, "Because I said!" The gap between you and a one-year-old is nothing compared to the gap between you and God. It's like the gap between Job and those two beasts and the beasts and God. God is so, so much bigger. It's not because we're unintelligent, but we are just people. We look at life through a little straw, and God sees the panoramic picture. So before we get all big and start questioning the love of God or trying to understand why something is happening, you and I need to realize we can't. We're nowhere as big as God.

So before you demand a reason why, let's not forget

who. You and I are small. You are not a big deal, and neither am I. Remembering that fact might just help you hold on to your faith when life is hard. Job said, "I repent. I despise myself for saying what I said. I repent in dust and ashes because I spoke of things I did not understand, things too wonderful for me to know."

Remember who you are. But even better, number two, remember who God is. He is the God of the mightiest storm. He is the Creator of the behemoth and the controller of the leviathan. He is the God, according to Jesus, who knows the number of hairs on your head; he doesn't

GOD USED HIS BIGNESS TO BLESS US.

have to guess. He knows every time a sparrow falls and dies. He has a name for every star when you stare up at the sky like Job; he knows all of it. And best of all, he did not use his knowledge to gloat; he used his character as God to save very small people, incredibly sinful people. God used his bigness to bless us; that's who God is.

I recently read a story about a guy named Dave who was diagnosed with brain cancer. It was terminal, and seven months after the diagnosis, he would take his last breath. He and his wife, Sharon, were a Christian couple. So during his final days, Sharon would sit next to his bed and hold his hand and caress his hair and talk about the God they believed in. But one day, one of their family members who did not believe in this big God showed up. He saw the suffering, and he got mad. He knew Dave and

Sharon; they were amazing people. They didn't deserve this. He knew Sharon was about to be a widow at way too young of an age; she didn't deserve that. He knew they had children and these children would go through milestone moments of life without Dad there to love them, to guide them, to impart wisdom to them. He got angry when he saw the senselessness of the suffering, and he snapped. He actually said to Sharon, "Sharon, why aren't you angry?" And this was her response: "My husband deserved to go to hell, but now he is going to heaven. In his mercy, my God forgave my husband because of the life and the death and the resurrection of Jesus. You want me to be angry? How can I be angry at God for taking my husband to heaven?"

Boom. That's who God is. When you and I think too much of ourselves—"I'm such a good person, I deserve an easy life, I shouldn't have any suffering, of course there's a place in heaven for me"—life is going to be hard. Faith is going to be hard. You'll think you deserve more, but if you realize that despite all you've done, God still loves you, it will change the way you see suffering. You'll start to say things like, "I deserve the worst. I might have a hard road for 50, 60, 100 years on this earth, but I have an eternity in the presence of God where there is no pain. I don't deserve that." In fact, the why questions you start to ask will flip on their heads. You'll start to say, "God, why would you care about me? God, why would my life mean anything to you? You're God. You name the stars, run the universe, keep atoms working like they should.

Why do you care when I pray about cancer or anxiety or a job application or a test? You're God. Why do you listen? Why do you keep loving me? My sins are so many. I get frustrated with me. Why did I say that? Why did I beat myself up in the car on the way home after a party because I said really dumb things? Why don't you turn on me? Why don't you get sick of me? Why don't you throw up your hands and walk away from me? God, why do you love me? Why did you send Jesus for me? Why did Jesus come and give his life for me? Why would you care? When I strayed, why did you come after me? When I was lost, why did you find me? When I wanted nothing to do with you and you just used whatever to draw me to the church, to your Word, to your Son, why would you want me?"

God's answer is: "Because I'm God. That's Who." One day, if you believe in Jesus, you will get to heaven. And I might be guessing at this point, but I don't think when you see God you'll ask him why. You will fall down on your knees and worship him for being Who. You're not going to spend your first semester in the presence of glory in Why 101 class where God will have to prove to you that there was a good reason. No, when you see him, when you experience his goodness, when you have that first hour of no pain or suffering or brokenness, when you realize that God is brilliant and holy, that you don't deserve to be there but he has brought you there—you will not ask him why. You will just thank him for being Who.

So the next time the devil messes with your faith, you

can say this: "Why is this happening? I don't know why, but I know who I am. A sinner. I don't know why, but I know who God is—my Savior." Remember who, and you won't need a why.

PRAYER

Dear God, thank you so much for your amazing grace and mercy. I can't see in this moment what you see because you see to the end of the story. You see all the things the enemy means for evil and how you will turn them for good. God, if I had the answer, I would trust you completely. But God, for some reason, you don't reveal it. I still want to trust you completely. Fix my eyes on Jesus, who came into this world to give his life for me to prove what kind of God you are. Help me remember that if you are the God who did not spare your only Son but gave him up for us all, how will you not graciously give us what we need?

God, I don't need an answer. I just need more of you. Open the eyes of my heart to see you like Job saw you. Help me grasp, as I look around at the glories of nature and especially as I see the brilliant things in your Word, what kind of God you are: A God whose mercy is more. A God of unfailing compassion. A God of limitless love. A Jesus Christ who is my cornerstone. You're all I need. Help me remember that. Help me worship my way through this struggle, through this valley, until I see you face-to-face. I hold on to you today because you are worthy of it. I ask this all in the mighty, powerful name of Jesus. Amen.

FOR FURTHER STUDY: GOD'S NONANSWER IS THE ANSWER?
DR. BRUCE BECKER

The book of Job is about pain and suffering. For 35 chapters, Job and his friends argued about why Job was suffering. Was Job bad? Was God bad? They couldn't figure it out. So in chapters 38 through 42, the Lord comes down to earth and has a face-to-face conversation with Job.

> **Then the LORD spoke to Job out of the storm. He said: "Who is this that obscures my plans with words without knowledge? Brace yourself like a man; I will question you, and you shall answer me."** (Job 38:1-3)

What was the significance of the Lord coming to Job in a storm?

What did the Lord mean when he used the phrase, "words without knowledge"?

What follows next are 77 questions that the Lord asked Job to answer. Open your Bible or a Bible app on your phone and read through chapters 38-41.

Jot down the various broader categories or aspects of God's creation (i.e., the weather, 38:22) about which the Lord questioned Job. See how many you can list.

How many of the 77 questions were you able to answer? Does your answer suggest anything to you?

What's your favorite or most interesting question the Lord asked of Job? What makes it your favorite?

A little more than halfway through the Lord's rapid-fire questioning, Job speaks. He makes a confession: **"I am unworthy—how can I reply to you? I put my hand over my mouth. I spoke once, but I have no answer—twice, but I will say no more"** (Job 40:4,5).

What did Job acknowledge about himself?

What did Job acknowledge about the Lord?

What was the Lord trying to accomplish with his questions

of Job? (Hint: See page 131, the paragraph beginning with "That's what God is doing with Job.") Did you notice that the Lord never answered Job's why question?

After the Lord finishes questioning Job, Job once again speaks. He repents:

> I know that you can do all things; no purpose of yours can be thwarted. You asked, "Who is this that obscures my plans without knowledge?" Surely I spoke of things I did not understand, things too wonderful for me to know. You said, "Listen now, and I will speak; I will question you, and you shall answer me." My ears have heard of you but now my eyes have seen you. Therefore I despise myself and repent in dust and ashes. (Job 42:2-6)

What did Job acknowledge about himself?

What did Job acknowledge about the Lord?

The story of Job doesn't end here. The last 11 verses of the book are worth reading. Read Job 42:7-17.

What did the Lord have to say to Job's three friends?

What did Job do for his three friends?

What did the Lord do for Job?

Pastor Mike concluded this chapter and the book with these words: "So the next time the devil messes with your faith, you can say this: 'Why is this happening? I don't know why, but I know who I am. A sinner. I don't know why, but I know who God is—my Savior.' Remember who, and you won't need a why."

What are your thoughts on Pastor Mike's final words? Contemplate them for yourself or share your thoughts with others in your group.

What is the most significant takeaway from this last chapter for you?

ABOUT THE WRITERS

Pastor Mike Novotny pours his Jesus-based joy into his ministry as a pastor at The CORE (Appleton, Wisconsin) and as the lead speaker for Time of Grace, a global media ministry that connects people to God through television, print, and digital resources. Unafraid to bring grace and truth to the toughest topics of our time, he has written numerous books, including *3 Words That Will Change Your Life*, *What's Big Starts Small*, *Gay & God*, *How to Heal*, and *Sexpectations*. Mike lives with his wife, Kim, and their two daughters, Brooklyn and Maya; runs long distances; and plays soccer with other middle-aged men whose best days are long behind them. To find more books by Pastor Mike, go to timeofgrace.store.

Dr. Bruce Becker currently serves as the executive vice president for Time of Grace. He is also a respected and well-known church consultant, presenter, advisor, podcaster, and author. He has served as lead pastor of two congregations; as a member of several boards; and on many commissions, committees, and task forces. In 2012 he completed his professional doctorate in leadership and ministry management. Bruce and his wife, Linda, live in Jackson, Wisconsin. Find his podcast, *Bible Threads With Dr. Bruce Becker*, at timeofgrace.org or on Spotify, Apple Podcasts, or wherever you listen to podcasts.

Pastor Michael Ewart serves as a campus pastor at The CORE, 922 Ministries in Appleton, Wisconsin. Prior to coming to Appleton, Pastor Ewart was a missionary in Siberia, Russia, for 12 years. He then served a cross-cultural congregation in Omaha, Nebraska. God has blessed him with a wife, six children, and three grandchildren (and counting).

ABOUT TIME OF GRACE

Time of Grace is an independent, donor-funded ministry that connects people to God's grace—his love, glory, and power—so they realize the temporary things of life don't satisfy. What brings satisfaction is knowing that because Jesus lived, died, and rose for all of us, we have access to the eternal God—right now and forever.

To discover more, please visit timeofgrace.org or call 800.661.3311.

HELP SHARE GOD'S MESSAGE OF GRACE!

Every gift you give helps Time of Grace reach people around the world with the good news of Jesus. Your generosity and prayer support take the gospel of grace to others through our ministry outreach and help them experience a satisfied life as they see God all around them.

Give today at timeofgrace.org/give or by calling 800.661.3311.

Thank you!